Running TOO Fast?

Creating Time To Lead & Still Have a Life!

Bob "Idea Man" Hooey

7th edition - Rewritten and Updated for 2014

"This is the beginning of a new day.
God has given me this day to use as I will.
I can waste it or use it for good.
What I do today is important, because
I am exchanging a day of my life for it.
When tomorrow comes,
this day will be gone forever,
leaving in its place something
that I have traded for it.
I want it to be gain, not loss;
good not evil; success not failure;
in order that I shall not regret
the price I paid for it."
Author Unknown

Dedicated to my award winning wife Irene Gaudet
who has invested invaluable time in helping
to make this writing project become a reality.

Dedicated to my fellow 'freedom fighters' who are
committed to taking personal leadership of their lives
and actions; who are focused on enhancing their skills
to better serve those they lead!

Preface

A number of years back I was driving home to Calgary from Lethbridge, AB early one winter morning. I had been working with Southern Alberta clients all week and wanted to get back to the office early so I could drop off my paperwork, get a bit of catch up done, and start my weekend. I was making good time cruising down the highway with the radio playing some great tunes. Then, I noticed a sign saying Castelgar, BC only 65 miles. Whoa! I pulled over and collected my thoughts. How could that be? I was heading home to Calgary, Alberta! Somehow in my overworked, tired brain I had driven right through Fort Macleod and missed at least two BIG highway signs reminding me to turn 'right', to head 'north' to Calgary. Sure I was making great time, but I was going in the 'wrong' direction.

Ever realize you were *'Running TOO Fast?'* - that your life was spinning out of control and your time was blurring as it sped by?

I love what I do and the people with whom I get the privilege of sharing my time!

Over the years I have had the privilege of investing my time and sharing my **'Ideas At Work!'** with a wide range of people. I've worked with front line staff, service people, professional service providers and sales people, professional association members, business owners, and managers. I've spoken and conducted training sessions, including one based on what I share in **'Running TOO Fast?'** across the globe.

I've found myself working more with leaders at various levels within associations and organizations as well as corporations. What I've found is many of them share the same challenge. They are TOO busy! They are tired!

I hear leaders telling me, *"...life is good; but, out of control, over-committed and with a blurring lack of focus on the important things and people in their lives."*

I've been there! I've been a 'freedom fighter' for years, working to recapture my time and take personal leadership over my life, goals, and actions. Over the years I have been able to help leaders and business owners become more productive.

This book began as a 'workbook' for classes I taught at several local Vancouver, BC colleges. It has been used by thousands of leaders and audience members in my programs across North America. Over the past 18 years, I've added tips, checklists, and forms that I have found of value to myself and my students. In this 2014 update, I've included some new tips and techniques I trust you will find of value in your quest to regain your life and enhance your leadership.

At the start of 2014, I decided to invest the time to update and do a complete rewrite of *'Running TOO Fast?'* My focus was to help my fellow leaders and their teams productively 'leverage' their time and enhance their expertise.

If you, as a leader, are TOO busy to invest time 'critical' to helping your team deal with their challenges, then everyone loses. I want to guide and assist you and your teams retake control of your lives by recapturing or repurposing your time. I want to help you become more productive, successfully grow, and profitably win!

We've even included a special section on ACTIVE Listening skills, a top performing leader's secret, just for you. When you invest the time to *actively listen* to those you lead (team) and serve (clients) they will help you become more productive and successful. It will save time and money as well.

This 7th edition of *'Running TOO Fast? Creating time to lead and still have a life!'* is my gift to you my fellow leaders and professionals. This is my gift to you and your teams in helping make your lives less stressful, more fun, and more productive.

If I can do it, so can you!

Bob 'Idea Man' Hooey,
Freedom fighter
& recovering over-committer

"Leaders (real leaders) gain their greatest satisfaction from seeing their team grow and win in their changing roles. That requires a strategic investment of their time!" This worthy goal is why we re-wrote 'Running TOO Fast?'
Bob 'Idea Man' Hooey

Copyright and license notes

Running TOO Fast? - Creating time to lead and still have a life!

Bob 'Idea Man' Hooey, Accredited Speaker, 2011 Spirit of CAPS recipient
Prolific author of 30 plus business, leadership, and career success publications

This book by **Bob 'Idea Man' Hooey** was originally published in 1996 as
'I'm Already Running As Fast As I Can!' and has been updated numerous
times over the years. It was rewritten and renamed **'Running TOO Fast?**
Creating time to lead and still have a life!' for re-release in 2014.

Cover design: **David Saxby**, Spark Communications,
www.sparkcommunications.com
Photos of Bob: **Dov Friedman**, www.photographybyDov.com
Editorial, layout and design: **Irene Gaudet**, Vitrak Creative Service,
www.vitrakcreative.com

ISBN 13: 978-1495999673 ISBN 10: 149599967X

Printed in the United States 10 9 8 7 6 5 4 3 2 1

Success Publications
Box 10, Egremont, AB T0A 0Z0
www.successpublications.ca
Creative office: 1-780-736-0009

Table of Contents

Preface 3

Copyright and license notes 5

Table of Contents 6

Running TOO Fast? *Creating time to lead and still have a life!*.....8

How to get the 'best' use from your copy of *Running TOO Fast?*.....11

Productivity tips 13

"I just didn't have enough time!" 15

A few dollars and sense ideas on Creating TIME to lead and still have a life!17

Potential areas of focus to help you create and save time...................18

Strive for flexibility and balance 23

Observing the speed limits of life 29

P*R*I*O*R*I*T*I*E*S 31

4 P's of Personal Performance..34

Stages of Employee Growth 37

Your current situation Leadership style 38

Each Life A Legacy – Live on Purpose!....................................39

Leadership skills are changing - are yours?..............................42

Qualities of an EFFECTIVE Leader, Coach, and Trainer.............45

Learn to Listen – A Leader's Forgotten Skill 48

Techniques to help you 'focus'..52

Creating TIME for effective training.......................................55

Accountability - key to effective meetings 58

Creativity is 99% perspiration and 1% inspiration 60

Be open and accessible to all ideas – regardless of size....................61

From 'KAI-ZEN' to 'I CAN!'

Improvement = Consistent commitment to good change...................63

The 21st Century version of the 3 R's....................................69

Confidence about Credibility 71

How much are you 'really' working? 74

How to use the information from your Daily Schedule Time-log

   or other check-up forms 79

Building blocks help make your life more effective........................... 81

How much is your time 'really' worth? 84

Identifying and eliminating your time wasters 87

Tackle your top five time wasters 88

My top five time wasters 92

Converting Filler Time to Foundation Time 94

Leveraging technology to get 'more' done 98

Meetings, boy do we have meetings 102

Value-based decisions 106

Secrets of a procrastinator - It's about time! 109

The POWER of UN-COMMITMENT!.. 111

Time wasters – the dirty dozen 112

How to avoid 'upward' delegation.. 113

'Carpe Momento' – Seize the Moment! 116

Bob's B.E.S.T. publications 120

Thanks for purchasing and reading

   Running TOO Fast? Creating time to lead and still have a life'!.............. 122

About the author 123

Acknowledgements, credits, and disclaimers 125

Disclaimer.. 126

What people say about Bob 'Idea Man' Hooey.................................. 127

Engage Bob for your leaders and their teams.................................... 129

Visit www.SuccessPublications.ca/TimeTools.htm for additional bonus pieces, just for our readers.

Running TOO Fast?
Creating time to lead and still have a life!

If you are like me, you may occasionally find yourself with too much on your already 'full' plate. You've said **'YES'** a few too many times, without fully counting the cost or realistically estimating the time actually needed to do what you've just promised.

- As a speaker, author, and corporate trainer, I am constantly tempted to take on 'just one more client', 'one more engagement', or 'just one more writing project'.

- As a leader, over commitment has too often impacted my quest to help my teams grow and succeed.
- In both cases, I often found myself staying up late to meet commitments or rushing from airport to venue.

Sound familiar? Welcome to the overcommitted club!

If this is just a momentary or *temporary* overload, you can dig in and work your way through it; or wait until you can get a handle on the commitments you've made. Then, you can relax, and get back to a more **normal schedule**. Maybe!

But, if this is your *normal life*, if you're **'Running TOO FAST?'** - then this book is written just for you! I'd suggest a long pause… to reflect and refocus, may be desperately in order. Take hope! You can make the necessary changes to free up your time for the important people and priorities in your life. It can be done and you can do it!

First, let's clear up the misnomer of 'time management'. Time **cannot** really be managed! We can manage others and ourselves in relation to time, but we cannot manage time itself. It will keep ticking along, slipping through our fingers like the sands in an hourglass, even when we wish it wouldn't.

Time keeps moving – we need to productively leverage our use of it!

We can control how and where we 'choose' to spend or invest our time. SELF-management focused on 'value-based' judgments is what is meant when we use the words 'time management'.

My experience has been that most people, especially leaders who want to make a difference, don't have the necessary skills in time management, energy management, life priority management, and planning to leverage for success. The truth of the matter is these 'management' skills are simple in concept and, with discipline, easy to build into your work and personal lifestyle. They work 'if' you apply them!

I found myself over-committed and overwhelmed and my productivity, energy, and enthusiasm suffered. I began to search for ways to increase my productivity and succeeded in stuffing more activities into my already over-committed schedule. I was killing myself trying desperately to fulfill my commitments and promises. I didn't want to let anyone down.

I found myself burning out from overwork, over-commitment, and a blurred lack of focus. I began to realize I needed to find ways to cut back on what I was doing and focus my energies and activities on what was truly a priority in my life and business. Over the years I have sought to apply these principles in both my life and my business activities. I have also gone back to the basics on numerous occasions.

For example, last year (2013) was for me, *'The Year of The Edit!'* where I strategically invested time to sort and purge both physically and figuratively. We merged two houses into one; a big move in itself. End result quite a lot of un-necessary 'stuff' and 'activities' (some even valuable) have gone by the wayside. My business and volunteer commitments have been reduced and refocused on moving productively forward and the office and commitment *clutter* has been drastically curtailed. We'll be doing this for Irene's folks soon.

I have taught these principles and brainstormed ideas on how to regain control of one's life across the globe. The lessons learned have helped tremendously in my own life and career. Along the way I have created time to lead some pretty successful teams, penned more than 30 books and success publications, spoken across the globe, and still had time for some fun as well as contributing to my community. So can you!

The time/self management techniques shared here can easily save you an hour or more each day. Think about what you could do with an extra 365 hours or more each year. The real question is, **"What will you do with those recaptured extra hours?"** Where will you re-invest them for maximum outcomes?

9

Take a moment: Decide right NOW where the extra time you free up will be re-invested. **Will your family reap the positive benefits of your better management of your time?**

Will you spend time building your self-esteem by preparing yourself to meet the challenges of our changing world? Will you choose to invest in honing your leadership skills and in helping others on your team? It's your time; why not choose to invest it wisely?

Bob 'Idea Man' Hooey, *Accredited Speaker*
Author, Leadership and Business Enhancement Coach
Bob@ideaman.net

In 2013 we invested several months updating and rewriting *'Legacy of Leadership'* in our efforts to help equip leaders and their teams to grow and to succeed.

We challenged them to **Strive for Significance – to Lead with Purpose!**

Visit www.LegacyofLeadership.ca for more information and to order your copy via Amazon

---

We offer a series of Leadership Success Packages to assist you in your leadership journey and to enhance your success.

- **Interested in Leadership**
- **Engaged in Leadership**
- **Growing in Leadership**
- **Committed to Leadership**

Visit: www.LegacyofLeadership.ca/Tools.htm to order

We also have a 'Leadership in a Box' package for leaders who want to work with their entire teams to equip them to take personal leadership and grow in their roles.

Visit: www.LegacyofLeadership.ca/Box.htm to order

How to get the 'best' use
from your copy of *Running TOO Fast?*

'Running TOO Fast?' contains a range of tips, techniques, and ideas to help you improve the way you recruit, train, and lead your team for shared growth and long-term success. It was not originally envisioned as a 'book', but as a course guide (manual) for programs delivered by the author in various Vancouver, British Columbia colleges and paid programs. It evolved into its present form with the inclusion of stories, ideas, and first-hand experience based on copious conversations, notes, and observations of productive fellow leaders. It was made personal from my own experiences in leading and being on a variety of teams across North America and the globe.

It has been updated with a focus to assist professionals and leaders to free up and better leverage their time to strategically invest in the lives and careers of those they lead. It is also designed as a timely guide for those who want to take personal leadership over their own lives and actions with a purpose of having their lives make a positive contribution.

This is <u>not</u> just a book for casual reading. It is a book to be 'chewed', to be dipped into, and leveraged as a resource or reference guide. It is a workbook with forms, surveys (homework); and, I hope, provocative questions that help you decide what you want to accomplish with your life, your leadership, and your relationships. It is your resource, so mark it, highlight it, and make notes in the margins.

To get the best from this book, first visit the Table of Contents to identify which chapters and/or topics meet your most critical, time sensitive needs. Read them carefully and make sure you understand the guidelines and advice given. Some of the topics may not be of direct interest to you (now) depending on your needs. You may wish to read some of the other chapters so that you can understand the needs of other leaders or scenarios.

'Running TOO Fast?' does not contain ALL the answers. It is a collection of thoughts, notes, clippings, tips, techniques, lessons learned, and ideas shared primarily from one learner, one leader's viewpoint, mine. It is simply intended as an aid to your reflection, learning, and inspiration – a resource that you can draw upon in preparation for your personal leadership endeavors. Its aim is to give you a creative resource that, when applied and practiced with real teams, will help you develop and build both your confidence and competence as a leader.

A more productive approach would be to take the tips and concepts presented here and blend them with your own leadership style, personality, and creativity. Keep in mind your own time constraints and 'comfort zone as a leader, business manager, or professional', to generate unique and personalized ideas on how you can create, give, and improve your interaction and action with your teams.

'Running TOO Fast? **Creating time to lead and still have a life!'** – 7th edition is designed to offer you flexibility in how you leverage it for your personal and professional use.

1) You can sit down for an hour or two and read it **cover to cover.** This is a great way to start by getting a feel for what is included, especially for newer or emerging leaders (those who want to take more *personal leadership* for their lives) who want to gain the full benefit from their investment.

A word of advice: *'Running TOO Fast?'* is the result of over 29 plus years of personal study and first-hand experience in a variety of leadership, coaching, and support roles for executive clients and their respective teams. It might seem overwhelming or confusing at first with the range of information included here. Once you have done a quick read of the whole book, identify particular sections or tips that interest you and work on manageable chunks.

2) You can select one chapter or section and work to incorporate the ideas you discover into your own leadership style and specific leadership role or personal situation.

3) You can look at the Table of Contents and jump straight to the tips or areas of study that particularly interest you.

We have attempted to incorporate something of benefit for everyone, regardless of your current level or skill in leadership. You might even find some contradictory advice in different parts of the book! This is because there is no single, universal 'right answer' – you must find what is a right fit for you, your objective, and your team's specific needs. What works for you is what is best. Choose it, try it, and adapt it as needed to serve you in your quest to be a more powerful and impactful leader and in taking control of how you allocate, invest, or leverage your time.

Productivity tips

Last fall (2013) I had the pleasure of spending a couple of hours with **Darren Hardy**, Publisher of *'Success magazine, What Achievers Read'*. Our discussion topic was how we could be more productive as leaders and entrepreneurs. This topic is very near to my heart and I took copious notes as he shared his ideas and stories with us. I decided to pass along a few highlights from memory.

He challenged us to say 'NO' more often and to narrow our focus and investment of time to the vital few functions that only we could do. Stop saying yes! He challenged us to cut back on where we say 'YES' if we were serious about our productivity. Darren challenged us to move from *'Reactive to Creative'* and to delegate everything we could to free up time for pursuit of what is more vital in our lives as leaders. Bravo!

He's met and interviewed some of the world's top performers for his magazine. He went on to share examples of super-achievers who successfully put these ideas into practice.

- **Sir Richard Branson** would work on only 3 strategic priorities at a time.
- Apple founder **Steve Jobs** learned the power of working on one BIG thing at a time and would focus for 3 hours on his number one priority.
- **Warren Buffet**, on average, only took 1 of 100 deals offered to him.

Darren suggested we should move from *'Labour to Leadership'*. He actually said everything we 'DO' is keeping us from what we should be doing. Hmm?

This rang true for me. I had just presented in Ottawa, Ontario at a national food and beverage conference for a group of club managers. I had challenged them to focus on what was the most critical part of their role and build on their expertise and experience. I had challenged them to invest time training their staff so they could delegate the less critical activities to them.

He quoted **Kenneth Cole**, *"Success has less to do with what we can get ourselves to do and more to do with keeping ourselves from doing what we shouldn't."* I looked down at my *stylish* Kenneth Cole watch (one of several) and smiled.

This too hit home, as I tend to be excited about ideas and making them work. I say yes too easily, often, to ideas which don't move my career or business forward. Point well taken, Darren!

He quoted from an interview with Steve Jobs where Steve said, *"I am as proud of what we don't do as what we do."* He quoted from one of my favourite management gurus, **Peter Drucker** who said, *"There is nothing so useless as doing efficiently, that which shouldn't be done at all."* Ouch!

He challenged me again, as a leader and entrepreneur, to determine my 'vital few' functions (that only I can do), my high impact priorities, and measurements to monitor and track my progress. This clarity in focus has helped in my quest to be more effective in what I do and in my pursuit to help my readers and audiences grow and succeed.

My plan is to do exactly that. I continue setting aside time to revisit my websites, programs, and publications with an eye to adding more clarity in what we offer and in what activities I engage in with our clients, colleagues, and community. I pass along his challenge to you, my new friend and reader; in the hopes that what is shared here in *'Running TOO Fast?'* will be a productive benefit for your growth and success as well as your life of significance.

Darren also shared these frequently quoted points. **Don't mistake:**

- Movement for **Achievement**
- Activity for **Productivity**
- Rushing for **Results**

I've heard variations of these, perhaps you have too. I felt they were worth repeating. Wishing you all the success and satisfaction in becoming a more effective and influential leader in your field.

 "Time is really the only capital that any human being has, and the only thing he can't afford to lose."
Thomas Edison

"I just didn't have enough time!"

Ever said that?

The harsh truth is, *'we have all the time there is!'* Each of us has the 'same' 1440 minutes in our day that were given to Bill Gates, Mother Teresa, or other famous folk. What makes the difference is how we allocate and leverage those minutes. Or, how we allow others to use or abuse these minutes for us.

In spite of a massive selection of seminars, notebooks, To Do lists, computers, and assorted electronic and paper organizers, we still find ourselves too busy and overwhelmed with commitments, obligations, and deadlines.

As leaders, being too busy to invest in working with, coaching, and leading your team can have drastic consequences for everyone.

We mean well, we really do! We even plan to buckle down and manage or schedule our time more effectively. Unfortunately, our human nature works against us, unless we make a disciplined effort to keep our lives and priorities on track.

The TRUTH – WE (not anyone else) are responsible for the gross mis-management of our time and the amount of time WE allow others to waste. We need to learn to say 'NO' to the distractions and the actions that take us away from what is our most important functions, the best use of our expertise, skills, and energies.

- What are we the **'best'** at?
- Why are we not focusing our energies on that **'priority'**?

We have all the 'reasons' why we didn't use our time more wisely or should we say all the 'excuses'. Sometimes the harsh reality gives us a wake-up call when we miss an important deadline because we procrastinated, overcommitted, or underestimated the time needed to finish a project and ran out of time. Sound familiar?

I've heard it said, *"Someone who lacks the will to say 'NO' will always be at the mercy of the time wasters."* There are always people who will take your time. They will steal it, waste it, poison it, and rob you of the very essence of your life; unless you take control and decide for yourself who gets how much time and for what purpose. Remember it's your time and it's your choice!

Today, you can decide to fight and take back control of your time and life! It takes planning and discipline, but it can be done!

One effective technique learned to help recapture my time and life was to set aside regular time to 'plan' future activities. A few minutes spent pre-planning each day, before starting, will save you hours! It is amazing what having a daily focus on the most important priority or critical activity can do to help free-up your time and stop saying yes as much!

Similarly, invest regular time weekly and monthly to layout and 'schedule your priorities' (vs. prioritize your schedule), block out specific times, and allocate resources to reach your personal and professional goals. This will make a profound difference in your leadership, life management, and the results of your time investment. It did for me, both professionally and personally.

Learn to **PLAN Monthly, SCHEDULE Weekly, and Lead Daily!**

Where are you on your personal time line?

0_____X_____ 10

0 = way far behind   10 = doing very well

Take a moment and give yourself an honest evaluation of how well you are doing in managing yourself in relation to the time you have to lead, live, and create a lasting legacy. Then ask yourself:

* What obstacle(s) stands in your way of moving closer to 10?
* What do you have to do or say no to doing to move your productivity and leveraged use of time closer to 10?
* When are you going to act?

 *"As you start to slow down, to cut back on your work hours, and to free yourself from some of your commitments, you're going to have some time on your hands. You may feel the need to start nourishing your body by catching up on your sleep, cleaning up your eating patterns, restoring your energy, re-establishing an exercise regimen, spending some time in nature, and learning how to laugh and have fun."*
Elaine St. James

A few dollars and sense ideas on
Creating TIME to lead and still have a life!

"Good, better, best: never rest till 'good' be 'better' and 'better' best."
Mother Goose

We've drawn from our *'Time to Lead, Manage, or Sell'* program in this update and rewrite of *'Running TOO Fast?'* The original pilot version of the *'Time to Lead'* program was designed and delivered for the BC Management Team of the St. John Ambulance, with all of their branch managers coming together in Vancouver, BC. Our objective for the session was a blending of solid leadership principles with a better use of time to allow their respective managers and their teams to be more productive in managing their efforts across the province.

It was very well received. I've spent time refocusing it, adding to it, and expanding it as a productivity tool to offer my clients and audiences in a quest to help them succeed. This program and success system is applicable for people like you; people, whose livelihood depends on your ability to take personal leadership, lead your teams, create and market our services, and sell them to your respective clients.

These tools and techniques work equally well for those of us in leadership, who seek to manage and leverage our time and the time of those who follow us. They work for those of us, who, as professionals, are committed to the Mother Goose quote (above) and work to improve on a continuous basis.

- How serious are you in making your career, leadership, or management a success?
- How serious are you in assisting those around you in finding success in their lives?

While flying to a speaking engagement in the US the spring of 2001, I read a study that indicated the average North American sales person puts in a 53-hour week. Yet, in spite of this long work week, less than 8 hours of face-to-face sales activity was recorded. WOW! Maybe that explains the lower results.

More recently, I read that the average North American executive or manager has over 40 hours (sometimes closer to 60 hours) of 'unfinished' work on his desk or agenda at any one time. WOW!

People are overloaded and it shows in their results and the outcomes of those they lead. Something is radically wrong with this picture. Work more, produce less is not a good indication for any organization which wants to survive and grow in the 21st Century. Certainly not at your organization; especially if sales and marketing efforts directly impact your income or revenues.

Working smarter is a better start; but working smarter **with** a process that allows you to cut back on your time while increasing both your productivity and profitability, is best. Saving time, blended with better leadership and management of time allocation, will help as you juggle priorities, and work productively to achieve enhanced business success.

Finally, it will bring increased satisfaction and better balance between your professional and your personal life. It is worth the discipline and work!

Potential areas of focus to help you create and save time

These productivity enhancing ideas, when applied, will free up anywhere from 1 to 4 hours per day. This time can then be productively 're-invested' in client and team interaction as well as in the sales, marketing, and management processes.

"No doubt over committed people find help in better time management techniques, but many of them will use their newfound skills to pack more obligation into their lives, rather than step back from their madcap pace." Howard Macy

Considering the average North American business/sales person works 53 hours and yet only spends an average of 8 hours or less than 15% of that time in actual client contact, think of the results of more time focused on this profitable area.

At the low end, what if you were only able to save and apply (2) two 'reclaimed' hours a week in the leadership, sales, and marketing process?

- What would an additional 25% surge in potential do for you at the end of each week or month?
- What if you could actually recapture and re-invest more than 2 hours a week in more productive activities?
- How would you and your team profit from that investment of time?
- How would you be able to enhance your family life and working relationships?

Time management needs to be an 'integral' part of your life

All of the tips and techniques we discuss in *'Running TOO Fast?'* or cover in more detail in our on-site interactive programs will be minimized without grafting a serious commitment and continuous action in time management into your life and work activities. They will work, but only if you apply them!

"If time and priority management is not an 'integral', daily part of what you *'are'* doing; all the technology/tools, as well as these strategies and time management success systems will be wasted."

Many of you are already 'jamming' too much into your hectic workweeks. The tendency for some of you will be to use these tools to crowd or load even more on your plate. This is counterproductive to the whole process. As mentioned, too many people will seek to do just that. I did until I burned out. Then I started looking for ways to free up my time and leverage my abilities.

The purpose here is to challenge you to decide what you 'value' and then create and schedule time for those activities and people you value. For some of you, this may be a welcome refresher and pat on the back for your efforts to bring your lives into balance and to make your career and business less of an intrusion. For some, this may fly in the face of what you've been taught or even the expectations of the environment in which you find yourself currently engaged or employed.

Please trust me when I tell you, it is all about finding a sense of 'flexibility', balance, and purpose and then applying that to being more productive in your life. Your career is only a part (arguably, a larger time commitment) of who you are and what you will do with your life. Ensure you factor in the important people in your life, as well as time to reflect and time to play and recharge your emotional and physical energies. Invest your time wisely, it is all you have.

Here are some time-tested tips, techniques, and principles to make effective time management a part of your life.

- Use a master task or 'big picture' list. Update, review, replace, and amend as needed to keep this current. Use this master list as a tool for your long term planning efforts and as a way to keep track of what you want to do, or promised to do. Then schedule accordingly to best use your time to fulfill your promises and to move your life and career ahead productively.

- Develop a 'STOP DOING List' of items you are determined to eliminate in your life and work.
- Invest at least 5-10 minutes in pre-planning for each day. Refer to the big picture list and see where these items might fit in your daily schedule.
- Carry over 'essential' items from your previous day's list; but remember, schedule wisely to avoid overbooking, or overload.
- Design a 'Someday list' as a place to park activities you can use as productive fillers while waiting.
- Design in flex-time for life's little surprises. You know - the things that get in the way of your plans. I've learned to never schedule more than 50% of any day which leaves flexible time for fill-ins.
- Use the method Andrew Carnegie paid a consultant $25,000 to learn. Rank tasks as A, B, or C's. A's to be done today, B's will soon move into the A category, and C's are 'done' only when you have time. Often, the C's can be deleted or delegated without any loss or even being noticed. (This works in helping you set priorities and then schedule accordingly.)
- Break larger projects into smaller ones and do a line chart with real deadlines for accomplishments. Put those deadlines and checklists in your daytimer or on your electronic calendar so they remain visible. Focus your efforts and work towards specific manageable tasks. Can you delegate some of them? As a leader, you simply cannot do everything. Think strategically and delegate effectively where applicable!
- Handle each piece of paper only once, if at all possible. Apply the 3 D's of time management: deal with it, delegate it, or dump it!
- Apply the 2 minute rule: If it can be done in 2 minutes or less – do it now!
- Use on-the-spot notes and documentation to adjust your priorities as needed. Do it NOW!
- Understand and use your energy levels and schedule for maximum output. Understand your biorhythms for best results. Know when your best time of the day is for creative or brain challenging work and schedule those activities accordingly.

Potential savings from making effective Time Management a focus: 30-60 minutes per day

 "Time is the coin of your life. It is the only coin you have, and only you can determine how it will be spent. Be careful lest you let other people spend it for you." Carl Sandburg

Would an extra 8 to 10 hours per week of recaptured or repurposed time

- Make a difference in your work day?
- Make a difference in your productivity?
- Allow time for more training and effective delegating?
- Help you with career advancement?
- Help you enrich your family time and relationships?

I frequently share these additional 'time nudges' with our audiences and readers with encouragement to explore them to see if they fit in their situation. Each of them works to free up or create *at least* 10-30 minutes a day by better use and leverage of your time and/or by eliminating or minimizing time wasters. Some even more! Not all of them will fit your use, but you might still glean an idea from each one.

15 minutes a day works out to approximately 91 hours over a year. 30 minutes a day is equivalent to 178 hours or 4.5 weeks. WOW! Perhaps, you can see where you might be able to better invest that recaptured time to grow yourself, your career, your team, or your business. Each can be explored and applied in less than 60 seconds. Good luck in your quest to regain control and leverage your time to be more effective.

These small 'seemingly insignificant' minutes, if reclaimed and invested wisely over the course of your life could easily give you the equivalent of an 'advanced' education in a field of your choosing. Would this make a difference in your career path? I would say YES!

- For example: if we read an average of twelve pages a day (about 15 minutes), we could easily read 17-18 business or leadership books per year. Considering the North American average is ONLY ONE NON-FICTION BOOK PER YEAR - you might begin to see the competitive advantages of investing 15 minutes a day in self-study.

- I've heard it said that, *"In one year, any one of us could become a local authority in our chosen field of study, in less than three years an expert, and potentially, in just under five years, an internationally acclaimed authority in that particular field of study."* Works for me!

- We enjoy a definite advantage or edge for success when we are well read. Reading BROADENS our experience, expertise, and expands our possibilities. Sadly, statistics show that approximately 40% of North American adults are not 'fully' capable of reading even their daily working material. Investing as little as 15 minutes a day could effectively teach them the fundamentals of reading and make a major impact in their lives and their employment prospects. We, as leaders, could make this happen!
- Alternatively, these same 'insignificant' minutes could help us get into and stay in shape while tuning up our heart. I'm told just 15 minutes of cardio-vascular (aerobic) activity - 3 times a week is all we really need to maintain a healthy body. Maybe take the stairs if it is less than two floors? INTERESTING! Only 15 minutes you say? Hmm, maybe tomorrow? ☺
- Perhaps these 'insignificant' minutes would well be spent or invested in personal meditation or spiritual contemplation, helping to bring your soul, mind, and spirit into balance.
- Maybe, these 'mini-moments' could be shared exclusively with your family or close friends engaging in real, quality communication to create and build healthy life-long relationships?

"Don't waste time," writes Australian pioneer Arthur Brisbane. *"Don't waste it regretting the time already wasted... you have time enough left (for some accomplishment and recovery) if you will but use it... while life and time remain."*

Your life and time management is 'truly' in your hands. It is within your power to choose to invest it well for your benefit and the benefit of those you love and with those you lead. Or, you can choose to let others rob you of your life's blood or squander it on useless pursuits. It is your choice - and it's about time!

A 60 second time nudge

Here are some quick reminders of effective ways to be more productive and make better use of your time. If you are a busy leader or manager, these will help. Are you are serious about increasing your effectiveness personally or as a leader and/or your income through building your business and team and finding ways to profitably create repeat buyers? They will provide solid guidance to increased effectiveness and productivity.

Consistent application in using your time wisely will allow you to free up time for face-to-face interaction with current and potential clients; as well as working with employees to allow more time for the leadership and management process.

This 'liberated' time can be leveraged in investing in equipping and motivating your team to win. Lead by example and get your team to apply these reminders to help them be more effective.

Strive for flexibility and balance

Above all in the process of learning to effectively leverage your time, strive to find and maintain a flexible balance between your personal and business time. This is crucial to your long term success! This is the only way you will find a sensible path that allows you to be productive, make the necessary changes needed to regain control of your life, and not burn out yourself, your colleagues, or your family members.

Potential savings from making Self/Time Management a focus: 30-60 mins per day

Strive for personal organization

Keep focused on what is an important 'priority' for you in each area of your life and career. Create your own 'Focused Five' list (where you outline the 'single' most important action that will move that area or priority productively ahead. (See page 32 for more). Start each day with time focused on planning and scheduling what is truly of value for that day. Schedule your priorities!

Remember: schedule around your personal energies to ensure the most important and creative activities are scheduled for that time when you are at your best. Time management is really a personal leadership choice!

Potential savings from better organization: 15-20 mins per day

Configure your office for maximum productivity

Your on-site productivity starts with making sure your working environment is ergonomically designed and organized. Reduce the chances of repetitive strain injury (RSI) or long-term loss of energy by ensuring things are within easy reach and located where they offer you the best efficiency. Over the years I have learned the value of a well organized work place where I can easily access and find what I need without needless wasted time. This one area alone can free up large blocks of time, a minute here and a minute there.

Potential savings from better use of design: 10-30 mins per day

Learn and leverage using technology

With the advent of improved and cost effective computers, printers, software, office networks, cell phones, etc we finally have access to a group of tools we can use to free up time. If you are looking for a competitive edge, you will find it by exploring and expanding your use of technology to systemize your business and reduce the repetitive activities to a minimum. This is an area where you can design systems or access apps and programs which will allow you to free up and leverage larger increments of time. Leveraging this area has allowed me to expand my ability to create programs and products to better serve my audiences and clients around the world.

Potential savings from leveraging technology: 15-30 mins per day

Use your website wisely

The smarter business leaders are learning how to more fully unleash the power of the Internet and harness the power of their websites by turning them into virtual assistants. Use your website as a client service tool, an information and resource base for potential and current clients; one that can show your potential clients the depth and scope of your skills, services, and commitment to their success.

Our **www.ideaman.net** website has been consistently revamped to do just that and it is paying for itself every year with client contact and contracts. Plus, we haven't even added the retail component yet. A few years back we asked some of North America's top experts to share their thoughts in *'A Creative Collection of Wisdom and Writing'* and have expanded the meeting planner section to offer assistance and free downloadable meeting and conference checklists, tips, and techniques from the experts. We've added article sections to **www.SecretSellingTips.com, ww.AlbertaSpeakers.com, www.AccreditedSpeakers.com** sites as well. Invest a few minutes to review some of the articles we've included from experts around the globe.

Potential savings from web wisdom: 15-30 mins per day

Use your email effectively

Investigate ways of harnessing email to provide ease of access to clients, using auto-responders to answer common questions and develop more effective ways of maintaining and initiating a true two way communication with your suppliers, colleagues, and clients.

Allocate specific times to access and respond to your email. Limit replies to one per minute. Use spam filters and create rules (which move regular emails from one source to a folder for later reading. Create contact groups for group emails. Create folders for newsletters and other regular emails. Read later!

Potential saving from better use of email: 15-30 mins per day

Maximize leveraging time by collaboration

As you learn to leverage your time, do what other successful business leaders are doing in increasing numbers – find and engage outside help. Use the services of a virtual or real-time assistant. Look for ways to outsource repetitive and non-revenue generating and marketing activities.

Perhaps you can work with a partner or colleague and share the load or engage a part timer who is tasked to free you up for those activities which potentially put you in front of those who can hire or buy from you.

Potential savings from not doing it alone: 15-30 mins per day

Leverage your marketing/promotion with assistance from others

A few years ago, I returned from our annual Canadian Association of Professional Speakers convention after investing a weekend with 340 fellow speakers, trainers, and facilitators. One of the speakers reminded us that we were first a marketer, secondly a businessperson, and thirdly a speaker. If you are not marketing, you are marking time; and if so, it is only a matter of time until you are marked for failure.

Focus on the most productive form of marketing and promotion – your sales and service efforts. Each client you sell and then successfully satisfy can become a marketer for you and your services. Each client who continues to visit or do business with you can become a fan and champion on your behalf. Ask for help in the other areas, such as networking, advertising, direct marketing, and public relations.

Nine years ago I created the first of a series of online promotional websites as a contribution to helping some of my colleagues work together to better reach our potential clients. www.AlbertaSpeakers.com has been very successful over the years, as have the other joint venture promotional websites such as www.AccreditedSpeakers.com

Potential savings from better marketing efforts: 10-30 mins per day

Leverage your time by better use of outside services

When you are busy and productively investing your time in the service process, make sure you work to minimize other activities that would distract you or deplete your time and/or energy. This one might be a more personal tip to free you up for more productive investment of time in your career role or in a leadership role in equipping your team to productively grow.

Look for ways to offload personal activities using shopping services, personal assistants, cleaning services, etc. Use the Internet to its full advantage for services and products you need for your business and personal life as well. Many office supply services will deliver to your desk if your order meets certain levels. When you consider the time and expense of shopping personally, it just doesn't add up.

Potential savings using available services: 15-20 mins per day

Plan monthly (or quarterly), schedule weekly, and LIVE daily!

I have been preaching this focused formula around the world for the last 15 years. My experience and those of thousands of my readers and audience members has been to use this formula as a strategic freedom tool.

- When I know what is truly important to me and am clear and honest with my values, I can say **'NO'** to things that do not fit my priorities and say **'YES'** to those who do.
- Take regular time either monthly or quarterly to think, reflect, dream, and then focus to gain freedom and to see your life become more productive, flexible, and balanced.
- Take the results of that process one step further and use that information to schedule specific time for strategic activities on a weekly basis to systematically achieve your goals.
- Personally, it frees me up to live and better enjoy my life *(on and off the job)* on a daily basis. I would hope it would serve that purpose for you.

One more tip in using your time wisely: Manage the mornings!

My friend **Wayne Cotton** challenged me to manage my mornings. If it is important and crucial to your success and long-term growth – schedule it and tackle it first thing in the morning. Then move on to what ever else needs to be done. That way, 'when' life happens, you have already accomplished your most important activities and 'high value' priorities.

This list of reminders or time 'nudges' can help keep you on track as you seek to grow yourself and your team to the next level. Accomplishing this challenge will demand your continued diligence in getting the best results or 'payback' from your investment of time and resources.

Investing those resources and the 'liberated' time with your team will help you reach this success.

More importantly, as you use these nudges to free up or recapture time (5 to 15 min blocks) make sure you know where you are going to reinvest this newly **found** time. As mentioned, deciding in advance where you will reinvest is a strategic move and one that will enhance your abilities to grow and to leverage your time for increased success and profitability. It will also allow you to inject a bit more fun in your life too!

SUMMARY

What this means, conservatively, is we stand to gain at minimum 2 full hours per day by better planning, leveraging and use of our time using some of these ideas.

Total time potential savings

- **Minimum 140 mins (2 hours 20 mins)**

- **Maximum of 270 minutes (4 hours 30 mins).**

As leaders, this is critical to your success and having the time for interaction, strategic training, and leading your various teams. This could be the most value added activity you could do as a leader. As a leader, would it be valuable to be able to invest the time in encouraging your star performers and coaching those who can be developed into stars?

As professionals, these time savings, if re-invested in marketing efforts, will dramatically raise your profile, your profits, and the quality of your life style. Scheduling creative time to think, plan, and set new strategic initiatives into action is critical to your ongoing career growth and success.

This 'recaptured' time, when wisely re-invested and leveraged in the management process, would give you a nice return on your efforts. Even if you were only able to average a better use of time resulting in two additional hours in only four of your five workdays, you would effectively free up eight hours. This would potentially double your time with clients, which could double your business as well as enhance your productivity. It would also open up time to effective engage your team members and help them grow to better success.

Pause for a few minutes and reflect on your answers to the following questions in relation to 'your' recaptured time.

- Would that 'recaptured' time make a difference in your take home pay this year? How much?

- Would that 'repurposed' time make a difference in your overall production and enhance your career or advancement potential?

- Would that 'refocused' time make a difference in your team's performance figures for the year? How much? Be specific!

- Would it make sense to continue systemizing processes or engaging the process of 're-designing' your work environment to free up this time?

- Are there areas where you can tighten up or re-design your schedule to free up time? Jot them down.

- Would some of these tips help members of your team to free up their own time for more productive use?

- Can you see the value this time leverage might have for you personally in your current leadership role?

- Would this allow you to spend more time training and delegating to free up even more tactical time for strategic use?

- Would this 'reclaimed' time allow you to invest quality time with your family and friends to build and enhance your relationships?

- Would this 'newly found' time allow you to inject more flexibility and fun into your life?

- What is stopping you from making these timely changes?

 "He who every morning plans the transactions of that day and follows that plan carries a thread that will guide him through the labyrinth of the busiest life. But where no plan is laid, where the disposal of time is surrendered merely by chance of incidence, chaos will soon reign." Victor Hugo

Observing the speed limits of life

Most of us, if given enough time to think about it, would be able to determine what truly enriches our lives, what makes us happy, gives us joy and a sense of purpose, or pastes a grin on our chin. Our problem – most days we are driving or running too fast to even notice. We're so busy working overtime, meeting deadlines, chasing career opportunities, and running yellow lights that we don't notice. The things we value, the people we love, that bring true riches to our lives, are often lost in the blur.

The hectic pace at which we live is costing us more than we realize; often what we say we value the most! As we crowd each day with more work and activities than it can suitably hold, a heavy penalty is extracted for resisting our impulses to rest. *"If I can only get this project done, if I can only land this contract, if I can only…then I can rest."* As a speaker, I am constantly stretched in this area. Left in our wake, amongst the swirling dust are our friendships, our health, our family, and our connection with our Maker. One reason I am passionate about this - it doesn't have to be that way!

When I was somewhat younger I remember saying (after watching my folks and some in their age group in retirement) that **"I'd rather burn out than rust out!"** *Boy was I wrong and arrogant too! That attitude and the speed in which I, like many of my generation, pursued my dreams and career; led me to a premature burn out and the loss of a marriage and a profitable business I loved. A harsh lesson to be learned for not observing the speed limits in my life.*

We are living and running too fast and the casualties are piling up along our causeways. In light of the economic melt-down in 2008, people are under more pressure to perform; to do more with less. Leaders are pressured to increase production with a reduced or stagnated workforce. It takes it toll.

Our excessive speeding is having an impact on our families and those we love most…our kids. It is killing our communities. It is killing our joy and on-the-job satisfaction.

People hardly have time to stop and talk with their neighbors anymore. Been broken into lately? Wonder why no one saw anything? No one was home! We were all so busy speeding off to a meeting or to work.

Slowing down in a speeded-up world is **not** quitting your career nor is it 'abandoning' your dreams or your desire to provide for your family. In fact it is how you achieve real success. Making an impact in this world requires that we slow down at least long enough to focus on the things which matter most and the people we love.

There are times when we simply must grab the wheel, gulp our lattes, and drive. But more importantly, there are times when it is deadly serious to pull over in a rest stop and relax for a while. To pull over and take a walk, to think and reflect on our life and our destination; to make sure we are actually heading in the right direction. We may be making good time and progress. But, are we working towards a goal that matters to us, that make sense for our families, and that adds value to our communities?

Pull over and give that question some thought! You will be glad you did!

 "Lost wealth may be replaced by industry, lost knowledge by study, lost health by temperance or medicine, but lost time is gone forever." Samuel Smiles

---

Taping into the power of making lists

Making lists can be one of the most productive or frustrating things you do. Some productive lists to add to your already 'overfull' To Do one.

- **BIG Picture list:** this is where you can outline all the items you have on your lists, so you can see where they fit.
- **Stop doing list:** actions or activities that you will delete from your agenda; actions that you are committed to stop doing.
- **Projects list:** a collection of all projects on your agenda (big picture of where you are already committed.
- **Next Action list:** with sequential steps or actions on a project.
- **Waiting for list:** parking lot of items you need to move forward or items that others need to do before you can complete yours.
- **Calendar list:** simple dates and deadlines for meetings, activities, projects, and other scheduled activities or commitments.
- **Someday list:** is where you park all those items or activities that you just never seem to have time for… if you do have some time open up you can check here and pick one to complete.
- **Bucket list:** might be a good idea for dreams and adventures.

P*R*I*O*R*I*T*I*E*S

"A hundred years from now it will not matter what size my back account was, the sort of house I lived in, or the kind of car I drove... but the world may be different because I was important in the life of a child." Anonymous

One helpful suggestion in your life and time management might be investing time to ensure you are 'crystal clear' on your priorities in life and business. Remaining focused on the priorities in your personal and family life makes it easier to balance and blend them with the demands of your business, community and career priorities. Far too many of us have personally paid the price for being unbalanced in our priorities and have lost partners, careers, and families. These needless personal tragedies could have been avoided, if we'd only invested the time!

Someone challenged me, that to be truly effective in my life I should begin to 'schedule my priorities instead of just prioritizing my schedule'. This subtle change in focus has made a major difference in its results and the accompanied lifestyle benefits.

Knowing what your priorities are, and scheduling specific time each week to work on them brings freedom. It helps you say 'NO!' to demands that don't fall in line, or would distract you from seeing your priorities fulfilled. You are better informed and able evaluate decisions, time investments, resource allotments, and specific goals. You can become more productive when you are working on the important projects in your career. You become more fulfilled when you spend time with the more important people in your life.

Perhaps spending a few moments on a regular basis revisit and revise your priorities would be helpful.

PLAN monthly, SCHEDULE weekly, and LIVE/LEAD daily!

Take a moment and make a note to yourself (yes, right here in YOUR book) about these various areas and your priorities. Spend time later to refine and focus your thoughts.

Keep your written priorities clear, concise, and focused. Keep them visible as you go through your day.

The following five have helped me keep focused. Update them regularly. Ask yourself, **"What is the 'single' most important activity I can do this week or today to help me reach my goals in 'this' area?"**

FAMILY:

SELF-IMPROVEMENT:

CAREER:

COMMUNITY:

SPIRITUAL/SPORTS/HOBBIES:

I routinely schedule my 'focused five' activities. I take a careful look at my goals, intentions, and areas of concern and schedule the five most important activities first. Then I schedule the remainder of my activities. That way, I am able to make important activities my focus as I work through my week. This has made a tremendous difference in my leadership and overall productivity!

You might want to add a few more areas or redefine them to help make it more focused for you.

LEADERSHIP: (specific to enhancing your skills and enhancing your productivity)

WORK: (separate from career)

PERSONAL: (separate from family and others)

If you've taken the time to fill out this section (and I trust you did) I'd like to commend you. Did you realize that you have now done what 95% of your fellow North Americans never have? Most North Americans have never taken even a few minutes to look at their lives and give some serious thought to their goals and values. And they wonder why their lives have been less than productive and fulfilling?

This time of reflection and refocus can be a pivotal point in gaining effective control of your time and life. Please take the time to pause and ponder your priorities. It is worth it!

TIME OFF - the ultimate perk!

Every year the Gallup, Harris, and Roper Polls conduct surveys to see what North Americans value highest. Since 1988 these polls have indicated North Americans wanted more time off to be with their families and do other activities instead of work. This was a major shift from the previous years. Sure has been for me!

- **How does this goal rank in your life?**
- **How will you schedule more time off this year?**

---

4 P's of Personal Performance

I've have the privilege of traveling across North America, sharing my thoughts and seeing my **Ideas At Work** on how to regain control of your life, leadership, and time. I've been able to share with professionals and leaders, just like you, and heard your creative ideas and suggestions on how to effectively tackle the problems and time wasters we commonly face.

I hear leaders telling me, *"...life is good; but, out of control, over-committed, and with a blurring lack of focus on the important things and people in their lives."*

Sound familiar?

Is there really an answer?

- Can we really take back control in this increasingly fast-paced world of high-speed Internet, cell phones, and other forms of instant communication?

- Can we balance our financial needs with our need for job, leadership, and family satisfaction?

- How do we balance our drive for personal and professional success with a need to actually live our lives?

- How do we create time to lead and still have a life?

"Success is not about money; it's about what you feel about yourself, your life, your friends, and your loved ones," shares former Success Magazine CEO **Peter Morris**. *"My friend, happiness, success, and enjoyment come from a balanced life, where material and spiritual values are viewed in perspective. The most profound success derives from the consistent application of your natural skills and energy in work that constantly challenges you to expand your horizons. Get a life!"*

The key here, as Peter said, is the word balance and a sense of flexibility. All too often we find our lives in an unbalanced situation. This causes the negative stress on our lives, our families, and our career. But how do we regain this balance? The real secret is 'simply' in how we portion out our time.

We've experimented with new ways of looking at and blocking out time. The results of this research are what we now call the **4 P's of Personal Performance.**

This planning process will, if applied wisely, help you re-focus your energies and resources in setting and achieving those worthwhile goals and the real desires of your heart. **As a leader**, please take heart, you can gain freedom by applying these techniques, along with the other ones we share in our programs and publications.

Our days can be more effectively used if we focus, plan, or block out our time, based on what I call the 4 P's of Personal Performance. Thanks to my generous friend Wayne Cotton for helping me expand these to make them more impactful with the association of color coding to make them more visible when blocked out. In brief, **here they are.**

PEOPLE/PAY DAYS: Our success in life, leadership, and business is often directly related to our ability to relate and work effectively with other people. As leaders our success is very dependent on maintaining good working relationships with our co-workers, employees, employers, suppliers, competition, and, most importantly, clients. **(GREEN)**

Simply put, a people/pay day is one where the 'major' time focus is on finding, building, and maintaining the relationships that are important in your life, leadership, and business. Investing time nurturing and augmenting these relationships can work miracles in team building, client loyalty, and business longevity. Hint: For the effective leader, a part of each day should be invested in this quest to better understand, support, and equip your team to win!

POWER/PAPERWORK DAY: There are days when the deadlines, the commitments, and the process of running our business and career just have to be our *major* time focus. Rightly so! The work has to be done, the business must be managed, and the invoices and orders must be processed. Power/Paperwork days, are the days in which we set aside blocks of uninterrupted time to focus on specific projects or obligations and work through to make sure they are completed properly and on schedule. **(RED)**

Days, when the work must be about the work, really do WORK! Hint: As a leader, this is where more effective direction and delegation come into play. Then you are freed up to accomplish your most important priorities and focus on your *vital* (only you can do) functions.

PAUSE/PLAY DAY: There are days when we need to regenerate, relax, take a break from our labours, enjoy our families, and sometimes daydream or even goof-off. Days in which we have fun, not focused on building a business or in pursuit of training that will advance our leadership careers.

Maybe we take a fun course in something unrelated to what we do – just for the joy of learning. Maybe we take part of an afternoon off and sit quietly on a swing or at the beach, watching the clouds as they slowly meander across the sky. **(YELLOW)**

Pause/Play days allow us time to reflect and refocus our energies, priorities, and resources and help make life worthwhile! They are most effective in helping us regain control and in balancing our power and people days to maximize our effectiveness. Hint: Build this into your current leadership agenda. **Darren Hardy** recently told me, *"As leaders, we should get paid to rest, to pause. Our role is not defined by what we do, but often by what we don't do."* He suggested a process of 'Sprint and Recover' where we work on one focused priority in 90 minute jam sessions and then allow ourselves to re-energize.

PLANNING/PREP DAY: These are days allocated, monthly or quarterly, to work **'ON'** your business or leadership, not **'IN'** the business. Days, when the 'primary' time focus is on strategic planning, analysis, and other functions of a long-range perspective. Hint: This is crucial as you seek to *liberate* time to become a more effective leader and help guide your team to more productivity and success. **(BLUE)**

Plan monthly, schedule weekly, focus, and lead daily!

That is not to say that you may have some weeks or days in which this isn't feasible or you are working your way out of being over-committed. There are days when you will only be able to accomplish part of your goal to schedule a people day, a pause day, or a power day. It is important to have a guideline to assist in effectively laying out your life and various commitments. Having a *visible* guideline also helps keep you focused and working toward your optimum effectiveness.

Enjoy your life and choose to truly live, to effectively lead each day!

Reminders to help you regain your balance and enjoy life

- "Just because you have the 'skill', does not mean you have the time!" Learn to say NO! In fact, this is one of your most important lessons if you are serious about creating time to lead and still having a life.

- Filtering your commitments through your 'life priorities' can be a very effective tool against over commitment. Ask yourself, "Is it 'really' important for 'ME' to do this?" (Don't do – Delegate!)
- What activities can you eliminate, delegate, or ignore to free up time for the vital leadership activities and people you really value in life? What's stopping you from being effective?
- 5 minutes spent daily on pre-planning can save hours in leveraged productivity. Plan and then do!
- 15 minutes daily invested in self-study or specific reading in your field of expertise can give you a major competitive edge in your career. A major investment that pays off big time!
- Use your day timer or electronic organizer as a strategic planning tool to block out time for leadership development, family, planning, fun, commitments and deadlines, creative time, and time for yourself. Control is a process of planning. It is a foundation for success in living and in seeing our lives become fulfilled and more productive.

Leadership styles and employee growth

Styles of Leadership

Director	Coach	Supporter	Delegator
Supervises closely	Coaches	Coaches	Hands-off mentor style
Trains	More supportive	Encourages	Leaves worker alone
1-way communicator	2-way communicator	2-way communicator	Listens - Facilitates

Being aware of the various styles of leadership and your preferred style will help you be more effective in working with those you supervise. What style leader are you?

Stages of Employee Growth

New Employee	Trainee	Skilled Worker	High Performer
Very enthusiastic	Becoming skilled	Very capable	Competent
In need of training	Frustrated with inability to be	Attitude varies	Committed
…and orientation	…more involved	Can be a problem	

Being aware of which styles work 'best' with your employees at various stages of their growth makes it possible for you to be more effective in giving them what they need.

Employees need different styles of leadership as they grow into their positions or as they move into new positions. An effective leader/coach realizes these needs and reacts to them in setting up a training and tracking program that is supportive and designed to allow the employee to win and become successful in their role. This forward thinking investment of your time can yield some pretty substantial return on your investment.

Your current situation

Employee name	Growth Stage	Leadership style

Exposing the 'myth' of Multi-tasking

Sure we can do it and do all the time. We eat and read or watch TV or we check email while on a conference call. And, we brag that we are more productive because we are doing two or more things at one time. WRONG! I'm guilty too. Truth is we are moving our focus back and forth between the different activities. More recently I have seen numerous experts who say it just doesn't work – or at minimum not well.

Since it can easily take 5 to 10 minutes to get into your rhythm multi tasking can 'actually' lower your productivity. **Here is an idea:** Why not uni-task on one item at a time. Set your timer on your smart phone, use a count down clock on your computer, a kitchen timer, or even an old fashion wall clock. Set it for 30-90 minutes and dig in. When it goes off, decide if you want to stop, continue, or switch tasks. If you've set it for a longer time (90 mins) get up and walk around for a minute before digging back in. Your productivity will increase and you'll have a great sense of satisfaction.

There are times when you can tap into multi-tasking, but being productive in your career role is not one of them. Focus on success!

Each Life A Legacy – Live on Purpose!

Our life and leadership is a portrait of who we are - autograph yours with style! Whether we realize it or not, our life and leadership leaves a legacy. People we know, lead, work, or live with will have a lasting impression based on their experience with us. Why is it we wait until they are gone to acknowledge the important people in our life? Life is a choice, as is leadership.

I've lived in the country north east of Edmonton, Alberta for the past 14 years. It is a quieter, rustic type of life. As I drive some of the rural highways I see scenes like this one. What used to be homes, inhabited by families with dreams. Homes left to fall apart, torn and worn by the winds and the rain. Homes left to the elements when the people who used to live there moved on. Houses, that have become interesting pictures of broken down buildings in a field. I wonder what happened. Yet, I see some older homes, lovingly cared for, passed on from father to son, family-to-family, still vibrant with life. As I drive though smaller towns I see vacant buildings that used to house thriving businesses. What makes the difference, I wonder?

What legacy will you leave behind? When your time is done in your current role, or here on earth, what legacy would you like to leave? What picture would you like your team, your co-leaders, and the community to remember about your work and/or your life? What would be the ultimate comment on your life and contributions?

Why not leave a lasting legacy that has contributed in a positive way?

Once we understand that we leave a legacy behind, we can make a conscious choice to make sure it is a positive one. We can choose to invest our time, resources, and energies in those activities and those organizations that create lasting value and in the lives of those we love and respect. As leaders, we have that opportunity to invest in the lives of those we lead. That investment can leave a lasting legacy in their productive lives and the lives of those they touch.

My parents left us in 1999. Their death left a big hole in the lives of my sister and me. But, more importantly, they left a legacy of love and commitment to community that has been ingrained in our lives. Their legacy lives on in our lives and our contributions.

Acknowledging the accomplishments and contributions of those around us!

Over the years I've learned that people all too often die unacknowledged and unappreciated. This is one of the biggest losses in our rich culture and legacy as a nation. We have people who have made an impact in our lives, who have made a difference too, and they don't know – because we never told them!

Resolve to tell people now and tell them often how important they are in your lives and where they have made a difference. It can be the most valuable gift you can give. This can be such a wonderful legacy as a leader – to tell people now how you appreciate them and their contributions; to share positive encouragement as they seek to grow in their respective roles.

Investing in the lives of others can be our best legacy!

I've often heard, *"You can't take it with you!"* Interesting thought! In one sense it is true. When we pass away we leave everything we once held important behind. *"I've yet to see a hearse pulling a u-haul trailer."* When we take personal leadership with our time and resources, we can re-invest them in the people we want to help now and in those who might be joining us one day.

Think of all the people who have invested in your life and your success to date. Some have passed away, but their investment in you is still paying dividends as you continue to grow and pass on what they taught you. You have that opportunity to 'pay it forward' for your team members, family, and communities. The most important activity and use of time is investing in our team for their success on the job. As leaders, this is our best gift!

Realize the impact you have and choose to make it a dynamic one!

We make an impact on the lives of others each day and in each encounter we have with them. We have an impact on strangers and on people who we may not even know. Like the ripples on a lake that bounce off each other, we do have an impact; and we change the patterns of those we connect with, as do those who connect with us.

One of the most decisive and productive decisions I made was to undertake to make a difference in my life, to leave a positive legacy behind me. To leave a legacy of empowered and encouraged people, audiences, readers, and family and friends who knew I loved and cared enough to give my very best. Who know I believed in them and prayed for their success and success in life. To make sure my words, written and verbal were based in truth, delivered in love, and focused on the positive opportunities in life. Thank you for investing your time with me in this personal leadership development book. I truly value each of you and the time we spend together over the miles.

"Lord willing, I have a few more productive years ahead. ☺ I still have book ideas to birth, countries I want to visit with Irene; and friends around the world I have not met as yet. But, regardless of the time He allows me, I pray that when I go, I leave a legacy as rich as those of my parents **Ron and Marge Hooey.** *I would be blessed indeed if I was able to leave that kind of legacy behind."*

What will you leave behind as a legacy of how you invested your time?

 "There are always two choices, two paths to take.
One is easy and that is its only reward."
Unknown

I believe this quote is from writer, **Mark Twain** who understood the full value of adventure in his life.

I use it to challenge my audiences to live their lives to the fullest; to think about what they do and don't do; and to plan and live their life with no regrets.

When we put off something of value (life) in trade for something of less value (work) we lose!

TWENTY YEARS FROM NOW YOU WILL BE MORE DISAPPOINTED BY THE THINGS YOU DIDN'T DO THAN BY THE ONES YOU DID. SO THROW OFF THE BOWLINES. SAIL AWAY FROM THE SAFE HARBOR. CATCH THE TRADE WINDS IN YOUR SAILS. EXPLORE. DREAM. DISCOVER.

(UNKNOWN)

Leadership skills are changing - are yours?

If you truly seek to be an effective 21st century leader, a reflective look at this list of leadership styles, activities, or attributes might be a good investment of your time.

As a dedicated professional, personal leadership is one of the foundations for ongoing and profitable success. So, even if you aren't leading a team, taking leadership responsibility can move you into the superstar lane.

- Ask yourself how many of these skills you currently exhibit as you seek to 'lead by example', those who have entrusted you with their concerns.
- What needs to change? If you lead a group of professionals this is an even more crucial piece of your puzzle.

Responsible: Do you take full responsibility for your actions and decisions? How about those actions of your team? Do you also take responsibility for their results, even if they are un-successful?

Growing: Are you an 'on-the-grow' leader, who is committed to seeking out new ideas, new methods and new alliances to help serve those you lead? Are you a leader who is also a strategic reader? Are you a leader who is *'Preparing Yourself to WIN!'* by equipping your team to win?

Exemplary: Do you walk your talk? Do your motives, actions, and attitudes reflect the character you would honestly like to become? What living 'legacy' do you seek to leave behind?

Inspiring: Do you inspire confidence and trust in those who follow you? Can you call them to action, in solving your mutual challenges? Can you get them to embrace and apply new ideas, methods, and opportunities to learn and grow?

Efficient/Effective: How are you at 'using your time wisely' and respecting the time of those you lead and serve?

Do they see you using your time in productive activities on their behalf? Do you have time to fully do your job? Are there areas of improvement in effective delegation and training to free up time to be more of a strategic leader?

Caring: Do your people know from experience that you care about them? Do you model it? How do they see this in action?

Communicating: How are you at sharing your ideas, at listening to the needs and concerns of your people and making sure that you fully understand them? Do you make sure they are well informed about what the challenges and your proposed solutions to those changes would entail?

Goal oriented: Are you a leader who effectively sets realistic, measurable goals; communicates those goals; and gathers people to support the attainment of those goals? Are you a leader who achieves the worthwhile goals set for the common good?

Decisive: Can you make an informed decision and action on that decision quickly? Do you study a challenge to death and continually put off making a decision while waiting for more information? Can your team expect a realistic response time to requests for action or decision?

Competent: This strikes at the heart of your ability to deliver the goods for your people. Are you competent to do the job and do it well? How is competence demonstrated? Are there areas where you are working on gaps to improve your overall competence in your leadership role?

Unifying: Are you a leader who seeks to include everyone involved and works hard to make sure no-one is excluded? Are you a leader who builds bonds between diverse groups and overlapping boundaries, many with conflicting agendas and viewpoints? Are you a leader who can earn their trust and allow them to get past their divisiveness and get behind you in accomplishing something in everyone's best interest? Are you a catalyst for commitment and creative change? How is that demonstrated in your actions?

Working: Are you a leader who is committed to working on behalf of those who trust you? A leader who is not afraid to get their hands dirty, to dig in and 'lead by example', to do what is needed, to get the job done successfully? Are you a leader who sets an energetic pace and is fully engaged on working out the solutions and to engaging people in the partnership of performance in achieving common goals?

Tough list isn't it? How did you do on reflection?

If you would truly seek to be an effective 21st century leader, these are the skills that will assist you in successfully serving and leading your people. These same leadership skills will help you win and keep your client's trust. That in turn will assist you in building long-term mutually profitable relationships.

What needs to change to hone your leadership skills and better serve your team, your clients, and your company? Are you willing to change, to lead?

 "Each morning when you wake up, you choose to take a step forward, a step back, or remain the same."
Justin Hazelton

Tap into the power of your mind

Taking control of your thoughts will assist you in making decisions that will help you re-gain control of your time and your life. Like exercise, this takes discipline; but it can be done and eventually become routine.

- **Learn how to ignore 'stuff'** – not everything deserves a response or decision. Don't waste your thoughts on unworthy decisions.
- **Idea Dump** – maintain an online or paper journal for the brilliant and/or interesting ideas you don't have time to work on 'right now'.
- **Apply the 20/80 rule** – leverage the 20% of your activities that produce the 80% of your results. Focus on the most productive!
- **Determine the outcome** – think through the process before you even begin. This will save you time and money and in some cases you might even decide to not do something at all.
- **Assume you are right – when in doubt.** Being decisive works.
- **Maintain focus on the important activities** – minimize the urgent.
- **Treat time as money** – be aware of your value and invest it wisely.
- **Write, then edit.** Be willing to do an imperfect draft. You can't edit an empty page or screen.
- **Visualize your end result or product.** Think it before you ink it!
- **Learn how to mind map** – creative way to plan or outline.
- **Start before you feel ready.** Avoid analysis paralysis in your work and life. Practice the art of the start! Better done than perfect!

Qualities of an EFFECTIVE Leader, Coach, and Trainer

Leadership is finding effective ways to bring out the 'best' from those you lead. It is finding ways to leverage their time and skills for increased performance and productivity. Becoming a good coach/leader means learning to draw on your abilities and skills to train those who need your help. Together you will succeed!

One lesson learned along the way: when we strategically invest the time to teach someone else we end up teaching ourselves. We also open the door for new lessons and leverage our abilities to succeed.

Here are some observed traits of successful and effective leaders, trainers and coaches.

Good communications skills
- Use clear and concise language to instruct, direct, and coach
- Use active listening skills
- Maintain eye contact

Solid understanding of the subject
- Comprehensive understanding of the subject or skills
- Willingness to draw from their background
- Willingness to grow and update their professional development

Good at leveraging and respecting time
- Their own time
- The time of those they lead

Experience
- It helps if you have done the job personally
- Previous experience or training

Patience
- New people can make mistakes while they learn
- It often takes a few tries to get it right
- Remember how it was when you started out?

Interest in being a trainer/coach
- Enjoy helping people

- Seeing people grow and learn makes them feel good
- Seeing others' success gives them a sense of pride and satisfaction

Genuine respect for other people
- People view them as being knowledgeable
- People view them as being trustful and trustworthy

Well-developed sense of humor
- See the humour in the situation
- Don't take yourself or life too seriously

How did you do in your self-assessment? Remember these are 'learned' skills! You can build them into your experience and expertise if you invest the time needed.

Having these traits and skills won't guarantee your success as a leader, trainer, or coach; but they will give you a better chance to do the job more effectively. They will also give your team access to a better-equipped person – YOU!

Building a great team - getting started

A word as we continue our journey in the evolving strategic leadership and management focus and on coaching in the market place or the workplace. As I am sure you are aware, the workplace is changing, as the marketplace expands to compete globally. This change in global focus places a new focus and pressure on finding and applying a more productive use of our 'time', resources, assets, and skills of our employees to compete successfully.

There is a definitive change in focus to using coaching in the workplace. In the past it was regulated or known as a 'remedial' method of helping employees improve sagging or deficient performance. It still has a valid use in this area, where needed.

However, recently coaching in the workplace has found a new value-added focus. Employees, managers and executives are experiencing the positive results from enlisting the help of a leader/coach to help them improve in specific areas or to achieve specific goals.

People have been going outside the corporate arena and enlisting or recruiting coaches because they want to change, to improve, and to win! Why not help them?

Executives and managers have also seen the wisdom and the positive return on their investment of 'time' and resources in training and in coaching their employees for optimal results. Things are changing in boardrooms and on the floors of businesses across North America and across the globe.

People experience problems and challenges in their performance for four major reasons:

- Poor or inadequate training
- Inadequate equipment
- **Time constraints**
- Motivation

Leader/Coaching in its core essence will help discover the area(s) that are acting as roadblocks for the person being coached. Coaching can help turn roadblocks into stepping-stones for increased success, productivity, and a real sense of satisfaction on the job. Coaching can bring a sense of satisfaction to the coach too - a sense of satisfaction in seeing your people win!

Let's learn together as you apply and teach what we share here in *'Running TOO Fast?'*

"Coming together is a beginning.
Keeping together is progress.
Working together is success."
Henry Ford

Tap into the power of 'creative' concentration

I shared recently, with my friend **Harold Taylor**, that I miss being close to a town with a coffee shop. I frequently get my best ideas and do some of my writing while sitting in the midst of all that hustle and noise. In fact, I will often play background music (no vocals) at home when I am writing. He told me that was not unusual. He shared that a recent study from the University of Illinois found the noise levels in a coffee shop actually helped some people concentrate and enhanced their personal performance. How cool is that! He told me there was a new website: www.coffitivitiy.com that allows you to bring the sounds of a bustling coffee shop into your office via your computer. I love it! ☺ In fact, it is playing in the background as I write this small piece. Thanks Harold!

Learn to Listen – A Leader's Forgotten Skill

Listening is the 'effective' leader's forgotten communications skill. Active, strategic listening is the secret skill applied by top performing leaders and their teams. This is the course you should have been given in grade one to help you succeed in school! This section will help you gain the edge both personally and professionally in your communication efforts. Your effectiveness will increase as you apply these new skills. This skill will help you and your team to enhance your productivity and succeed!

Some Listening Facts

If you are like most people, you spend approximately 60 percent of your workday listening. Like many of us, you probably retain only 25 percent of what you hear. In less than two months, most people generally recall only half of the 25 percent of the message they initially retained.

There is also a substantial difference between the average rate at which people speak (100 to 250 words per minute) and the time required by the average listener to process the message (400 to 500 words per minute.) This allows you to tune in and out of the message, which means you may miss the meaning the speaker intended.

If you are an effective listener and leader, you will use the time variance to anticipate what the speaker will say next, analyze the speaker's message, search for meaning, and review previous points the speaker made to reinforce their ideas.

Listening is an acquired skill – often forgotten in our rush to maintain our hectic and increasingly global business endeavours. Good listening skills pay off. Conversely, poor listening skills have measurable results, which are negative personally and professionally.

Three Factors Affect Your Ability to Listen

1. **Motivation is a significant element of successful listening.** Your comprehension improves if you are interested in the topic, if the message itself is interesting and entertaining, or if you know you are going to be tested on the content of the message.

2. **Organization of the message directly affects your comprehension of the message.** If you can organize and structure a message as you listen to it, you will understand more. Speakers who deliver the message can help by presenting it in an organized manner.

3. **Environment factors influence comprehension.** Have you ever let yourself be distracted by external noise, excessive fidgeting by the speaker, poor lighting, and a host of other distractions or problems that can arise? Effective listeners learn to compensate for these distractions.

Good Listening means ACTIVE Involvement

Content and attitude are two important elements in any verbal message that you, as an active listener, must try to understand.

Author Stephen Covey, says in his *'The Seven Habits of Highly Effective People'*: *"...you must listen with your eyes and with your heart. You must listen for feeling, as well as for meaning. You must listen for behavior. You must use your right brain as well as your left. You sense, you intuit, you feel..."*

Probing questions will help you improve your listening skills. Watch for visual or soft sound cues. Voice inflection, the use of ...pauses, and the speaker's expressions, posture, hand gestures, eye movements and breathing can provide you with help to understand the message. The following are excerpts from my Active Listening series.

ACTIVE LISTENING SKILLS

Good listening skills are important to any organization and specifically to your leadership or personal career! Listening is an essential part of the communication process in how we obtain, process, and pass along information. It is an acquired skill applied by top performing leaders to help their teams grow and succeed.

The communication process incorporates four basic elements:

- Reading
- Writing
- Speaking
- **Listening**

To begin, it is important to understand the true essence of listening. Someone once told me that, *"listening is to hearing, what reading is to seeing"*. Webster's defines hearing as, "to perceive or apprehend using the ear". Listening on the other hand is defined as, "to pay attention to sound - to hear with thoughtful attention".

How can good listening skills or lack of these skills impact your life, family or career?

The consequences of poor listening skills include:

- Lower productivity and morale
- Lost sales
- Unhappy clients
- Increased costs
- Lost profits
- Less effective use of time, people, and resources
- Relationship breakdowns and personality clashes
- Accidents
- Production breakdowns and wasted time and effort

Good listening skills:

- Help improve relationships
- Minimize serious misunderstandings
- Leverage use of time, people, and resources
- Improve communications between co-workers, management, suppliers, and clients

Learn to question effectively so you can be a more successful listener. Don't be afraid to actively get the information you need to ensure you've effectively heard and clearly understood the message. This part is your responsibility. Effective communication is a partnership between speaker and listener to ensure the information is accurately transmitted and received.

Why don't we listen, if we know the negative consequences and positive benefits? Here are a few ideas gleaned from class discussions over the years.

- Listening is hard work, concentrating on the other person and actively focusing our energies to hear and understand what they say.

- We have enormous competition for our attention in today's society with radio, TV, movies, written material, and the Internet clamoring for our time. We are overloaded daily with stimuli we have to process and prioritize just to survive.
- We jump in and interrupt, because we 'THINK' we know what the other person is going to say, thereby depriving them of being heard out in full.
- The listening GAP (listening capabilities at 400-500 words per minute compared to speaking at 100-250 words per minute) between the speed of thought and speech allows us to jump to conclusions, fill in the time with daydreaming, forming a reply or rebuttal, or work on other projects mentally.
- A lack of formal training; even though we do much more listening than reading or speaking. Many untrained listeners retain less than 25% of what they hear. This means effectively that 75% of what we hear may be distorted or forgotten.

We tend to listen at one of several attentive levels. While they tend to overlap or interchange, it is important that we be aware of these various levels.

- **Unconscious** listener: doesn't even hear the speaker. A blank look or glazed eyes, faking attention, nervous gestures, or constant interruptions accompany this level.
- **Superficial** listener: hears the sounds, but doesn't understand the meaning or intent of the words. This person is too busy preparing their next statement to really listen and is quite easily distracted by their environment.
- **Evaluative** listener: is trying to hear what is being said, but again not really understanding what is being meant or the intent of the speaker. More concerned with content than feelings, focusing on logic and responding to the message by evaluating the words delivered, ignoring the vocal intonation, facial expression, or body language which gives us the broader, more accurate message.
- **ACTIVE** listener: is a powerful listener focusing on understanding the speaker's point of view, paying attention to the thoughts and feelings in addition to the words.

Active listening means refraining from judging the speaker's message, suspending for the moment our own feelings and thoughts to get to the speaker's intent and message. ACTIVE listening is hard work, as it requires our attention and concentration; as well as mental and emotional processing.

Techniques to help you 'focus'

The following techniques will help you focus and concentrate, while listening. They will also help you counteract distractions.

- Deep breathing: whenever you feel like interrupting the speaker, take a deep breath… and listen! It works…if you're breathing in, you can't interrupt can you?
- Make a 'conscious decision' to LISTEN by paying attention and looking for interesting items in the conversation. Mentally paraphrase what the speaker is saying. By putting it in your own words you keep concentrating and help to prevent yourself from daydreaming. By echoing, evaluating, rephrasing, anticipating, and reviewing what the speaker is saying, you help yourself to concentrate on the speaker, not yourself.
- Maintain eye contact. Your ears will often follow where your eyes lead. Acknowledge the speaker by maintaining eye contact, smiling, nodding, leaning forward, facing the speaker, or using appropriate facial or body gestures to project a positive response.
- Clarify points by asking questions or restating the information, to ensure you've gotten it accurately. You may even use verbal strokes, like "really", "Hmmm", "go on" to help draw out the speaker.
- Be actively involved in research! By research I mean clarifying a message, enlarging on a topic, getting the speaker to change conversational direction, or prompting then to tell you more. This allows us to support the speaker by reinforcing particular parts of their talk.

Listening is part of a two-way flow of communication, which facilitates a meeting of the minds, and helps make the speaker feel more comfortable and able to open up.

- **Exercise emotional control** instead of focusing on the provocative aspects of a speaker's appearance, accent, vocal tone, vocabulary, or style. If we don't do this we may miss the true substance and meaning of the speaker's message.
- **Learn how to recognize and redirect negative emotional reactions.** Pause to delay your reaction, find common ground (i.e. what you have in common) instead of focusing on differences, and learn how to visualize yourself relaxed and calm. It helps!

Popular research has shown that only 7-10% of the message, the meaning, is actually carried through the words we use. Close to 90% of the message is conveyed through the vocal and visual presentation channels.

Someone once told me, *"In speaking…YOU are the message!"* This would be true as a leader too! This is not too far off the mark, if we consider the weight our audience places on the manner in which we speak and in how we present our message, compared to the words we use.

Three Methods. There are three methods which will help you actively listen to the content of a speaker's message, and prevent yourself from drifting off.

1. 'Comparing' between what is fact and what is opinion, between the positives and the negatives, between the pros and cons, and between the advantages and disadvantages.
2. Listening to hear 'if' the speaker is 'consistent' with his or her own material. 'Sequencing' is essentially listening for priority or logical order. Listen for transitional words like, 1st, 2nd, 3rd, or next.
3. 'Indexing' by taking written or mental note of the major idea or topic, the key points as discussed or outlined, and the sub-points or reasons and supporting points brought out by the speaker. Again, listen for those transitional words.

Make sure you hear and understand the words being used. This can be a major source of miscommunication between people; more so with our blended cultural backgrounds and experience. In North America, we have about 500 or so more commonly used English words with a potential for over 14,000 connotations or definitions. Perhaps it is possible for us to misunderstand the use of a particular word in conversation?

Listen in 'context' and check it out if you're not sure. Don't react emotionally or negatively to a word - it might not be meant in that manner. Check it out first - then act if necessary. This can be one of the most productive leadership/listening tips I can give you.

Learn to listen for the connotation, which is essentially what the word means through suggestion, context, or implication, rather than definition, which is focused on the dictionary meaning.

When we assign a different meaning to a word than the speaker we miss or bypass the communication process. It takes concentration to ensure we hear and understand.

We can develop an **Active Listening Attitude**, but it takes work and reinforcement. When we decide listening is just as powerful as speech, we begin to give our listening skills more attention.

Active Listening:

- **Saves time**
- Fewer mistakes
- Less misunderstandings
- Reduces customer or employee turnover, and frustration
- Helps us in our interpersonal relationships
- Allows us to suspend judgment for the moment
- Allows us to really communicate by hearing what is said, before we respond

When we truly believe that we can learn from everyone we meet, we begin to realize our listening skills are vitally important and worthwhile. It is worth the effort.

This excerpt is originally from a program in **Applied Communication Skills** taught at Langara College in Vancouver, BC for many years and was included as a 'foundation for effective presentations' due to its parallel leadership lessons and its applied techniques in helping understand and focus on our audiences and those with whom we interact or lead.

Your listening skills will prove invaluable in Q &A periods, reading the moods of those who are listening to your presentations, and in getting the information you need to effectively present your views and projects. They will help you in your relationships with family, friends, co-workers, employees, team members, and community groups. Additionally, as a part of effective communication skills, your improved listening will help set you apart in your career advancement. Leaders use active listening skills as a bridge to connection with their teams.

Listening is a critical success skill

I remember getting a call from a grade 5 teacher asking me, **"What did you tell these kids last week?"**

Evidently they had taken to heart my comment that **"Listening to someone is the ultimate gift of respect!"** made during my Toastmasters International Youth Leadership presentation with her class. Guess they got it and applied it. The results of this skills impact were proven in the actions of these young leaders! My guess, they will grow up more successful by applying this leadership secret.

Creating TIME for effective training

Investing in continual training and professional development allows your team the opportunity to fully realize their potential. It pays big dividends on better-equipped, energized team players on the job. As a top level leader and team coach this can be your biggest time challenge as well as opportunity for success.

Finding 'time' for your team members to attend training can be a challenge for most organizations. Applying creativity to your training program can yield powerful results in their sales and customer recruitment and retention.

These ideas will reduce excessive classroom instruction time, without jeopardizing the process of quality face-to-face, interactive training

- Schedule team members to attend training between 10AM and 3PM, instead of a full day. In this case they can still attend to urgent business and client follow up. This works well for on-site training or training held very close to your operation.
- Weekend seminars and retreats are increasing in popularity. However, if you ask your team to sacrifice their private time, be sure to include some group outing or banquet to show your appreciation. Trade off time during the week would be nice too!
- Suggest your team study or read up on the course material in advance so they can hit the seminar running. Professional trainers can provide advance materials to facilitate this process.
- How about scheduling a 'lunch and learn' or 'breakfast briefing with Bob' by inviting in a local expert when your team needs information on a simple topic. Or combine a 'breakfast briefing' for management or specific team members in addition to half day or full day training.
- Visit: **www.ideaman.net** for more information on our programs and materials to assist you in enhancing your career or leading your team.

How to avoid 'expensive' training mistakes

As a leading edge owner, executive, manager, or team leader you may be asked to make decisions to engage or contract on programs and policies that will either help or hinder your team in reaching their goals.

You can avoid making 'major-career limiting-expensive' training mistakes by considering a few ideas and side-stepping some of these mistakes that have minimized returns on training dollars. Unfortunately training dollars are ultimately wasted when leaders make some or all of the following mistakes. You can avoid them!

- **Failing to fully assess team needs**

Perhaps you are teaching your team skills they already have? Team members don't need training 'just for the sake of training'. I've heard managers say, *"Even if they know this stuff – a refresher won't hurt them!"*

Sometimes that is true (I have been asked back to reinforce a program or to provide add-on sessions or coaching). If not handled correctly, it can be counter-productive to your end goals or de-motivating to your team.

Here's a suggestion

Before you launch any training program, conduct a needs assessment with your team. Work to establish a 'comprehensive list of skills' of current team members. This way you may discover what they already know and what they need (and hopefully want) to learn. Then, as you provide training, it will send a 'positive' message that reinforces the idea that you value their contributions and are dedicated to helping them increase and hone their skills. Training can be perceived as a 'punishment or a perk' depending on how you position or frame it.

Strategically design your training programs to incorporate follow up reinforcement to enhance their effectiveness. Make that a vital part of your program and design it to ensure it is productive reinforcement not a perceived punishment. Let them know you are committed to their growth and success in their roles.

- **Thinking (wishfully) that training sessions will eliminate conflict**

Leaders and managers sometimes think that training, especially training that focuses on team or relationship building, will, in itself, eliminate conflict on the job. Some programs over emphasize team-work at the expense of 'team-effectiveness'. All team efforts need to be focused; task and relationship oriented. When sessions focus 'too much' on relationship building vs. team-effectiveness they lose impact and may become counter-productive.

Team building is a very important aspect of any successful business or organization. Make sure it is not 'sacrificed' in replacement for 'team-effectiveness'. Professional leadership is being able to work with people who may 'bug you' and being able to direct their efforts to help the team succeed.

Here's a suggestion

Work diligently to ensure everyone on your team understands that *constructive* conflict is an important part of the team process. Without some conflict and honest difference of opinion, you get mediocrity. As someone once told me, *"The opposite of conflict is apathy, not peace and harmony."*

The secret is in not taking conflict as a 'personal issue' or a negative result in the process. Creative, constructive conflict can be a 'strategic' part of a positive process in making sure your team makes the right choice and (time permitting) fully explores all the options and potential pitfalls.

Visit: www.legacyofleadership.ca/bonus.htm for a special gift to help you in your leadership journey.

- **Thinking of training as a program vs. an on-going process**

One of the challenges in training is the expectation that a half-day, full day or even a few days of training can change years of embedded habit. Research shows that shorter sessions, with reinforced follow-up, spread over a longer time result in better retention and long-range effectiveness. 'Short and often' rather than a one-time massive attack seems to work better.

That is one of the reasons behind the success of our spaced online video coaching and training programs like *Secret Leadership Tips* or our *Speaking for Success* on-line coaching series.

Here's a suggestion

For your training to be effective, insights and ideas gained during programs must be quickly translated into action (**Ideas At Work!**) – actions that are reinforced by the leaders on your team. Real development is never completed, as is the true essence of education. In our live interactive sessions, audience members are challenged to make a specific commitment to act on what they learn and to schedule those actions.

Visit: www.ideaman.net for more information.

We trust these suggestions will help you as you search out the most effective training programs for your team. We'd be happy to share some other thoughts with you if you have any other questions or queries. Of course, we'd be happy to explore how we might be of service in on-site training for you and your team.

Accountability - key to effective meetings

Meetings can be our biggest time drags. How often have you sat in meetings listening to 'excuse after excuse' from people who didn't do what they said they'd do at the last meeting? People who are not prepared for the meeting or who haven't even done their homework? How often have you led a meeting and heard excuse after excuse? Does it bug you? It sure does me!

One of the 'tools' used to help 'counteract' this frustration is a detailed action list (different than minutes) which summarizes what was agreed to be done, by whom, and by when. This accountability action list, is kept and circulated in a 'timely' manner to all in attendance 'immediately' following the meeting. It helps make people take personal leadership and be more 'accountable' for their actions or lack of action.

Two things will happen:

1) They will start doing more; doing what they've agreed.
2) They will stop talking and over-committing.

Either way you win!

Here is a sample basic **Action List** form for your consideration:

Name	Action or commitment	Deadline	Done
Bob Hooey	Finish rewrites and edits	Mar 16th	X
Irene Gaudet	Proof /edit *'Running TOO Fast?'*	Mar 20th	X
Bob Hooey	Send to printer	Mar 26th	X
Bob Hooey	Promote *'Running TOO Fast?'*	on-going	

- The first secret to effective meetings is to **ONLY** hold them if they are critical, relevant, and move the team and/or the project forward.
- The second secret to effective meetings is in a timely process of tracking and sharing accountability. That, coupled with setting your performance expectations high, can work wonders in any organization.

This leadership/team effectiveness accountability tool can be powerful when used properly and publicly. Just as in the secret of success teams, group accountability can push us to 'actually' complete that to which we commit. If the purpose for the meeting is important and vital to the success, growth, or other purposes of your organization or group, don't you think the follow through is 'just' as important?

This is even more important in volunteer groups where people with individual agendas come together under a common banner. The challenge is to blend or re-direct those agendas toward the common good. Then, having done that, to follow through and accomplish what has been discussed. Don't be afraid to hold people accountable and set a higher standard. Again, they will respond or they will leave you to accomplish that which is important. Either way, you win!

 "What we need to do is learn to work in the system; by which I mean that everybody, every team, every platform, every division, every component is there not for individual competitive profit or recognition, but for contribution to the system as a whole on a win-win basis." W. Edwards Deming

---

Harness the power of 'puttering'

My friend **Patricia Katz, CSP, HoF** shared this response to handling high demand, stressful times in her recent **'Pause'** newsletter. She'd asked for ideas. "This particular fellow described his stress reduction strategy as 'puttering'. He explained that when life and work grow demanding, he narrows his attention and focuses only on the high priority items.

But, after several weeks of that high level focus, he finds he has sidelined a whole pile of lesser tasks. These smaller, less important bits and pieces build up to create a pressure all their own. At that point, he devotes a day to puttering. No major projects and no big decisions are allowed. Instead, he putters around clearing away the small stuff.

He calls A, repairs B, stores C, answers D, files E, replaces F, cleans up G, and so it goes. As he moves from one small task to another with ease and a meandering spirit, he fuels a sense of accomplishment and feels a sense of relief." Loved this idea and got permission to share it with you.

© Patricia Katz, Used with permission. Visit her at: www.PatKatz.com

---

Creativity is 99% perspiration and 1% inspiration
"Who said it was going to be easy?"

Bryan Mattimore's excellent creativity book, **'99% Perspiration'** should be in your organization's library. Actually, it should be signed out and being 'worn out' by you and your team. This kind of reading would be time well spent preparing and priming your creativity pump. This is where the 'creative' and 'profitable' ideas come from in better serving your clients and expanding your career or business. This is where you create ideas to profitably enhance your productivity.

I've adapted this excerpt from our *'Create the Future! - Vision and Innovation'* manual as a sampler and perhaps a seed for your success in finding time to more productively grow your own leadership, team, and organization.

Our ongoing success and survival in business is directly dependent on our 'creative ability' to profitably solve the problems in our client's lives and operations. We use our innovative solutions to help make their lives and businesses better. Accessing or tapping into our creativity can be hard work, unless you systemize your approach.

We hear stories of the 'ah-ha' moments in history, business, and science. In reality these 'lightning bolt' or 'light bulb' occurrences nominally come about after many hours of research and applied study into a particular topic.

I know that is how it usually works in my writing and program creation activities. I research, read my brains out, and take copious notes, long before I start writing. Then I edit, have other people read and edit, and rewrite. Then I publish and take a breath.

Innovative ideas are sometimes 'mined' from lessons drawn from past failures. Consider **Thomas Edison** and the thousands of attempts to find a sustainable material for the filament for a light bulb.

Take the time to conduct systematic and well-rounded research, coupled with 'mining' the lessons learned from your errors and mistakes. This will help fill your mind with the raw materials necessary for creative process development.

This is, as you guessed, the 'perspiration' part of the creative process, and takes an active investment on your part.

During the 'incubation' period, let your subconscious mind chew on all this material. Let it forge new and varied connections with the seemingly unrelated bits of information. Your subconscious will then send these vague feelings or intuitions to the surface or conscious mind. The creative leader knows to capture these random thoughts, however vague, impractical, or wild for later evaluation and analysis.

Be open and accessible to all ideas – regardless of size

I've seen many people fall into the trap of waiting for the *big idea* – a completely novel idea for a product, project, or service. They sit and wait for sudden inspiration or brilliant flashes of insight. Many are still waiting. Focusing on big ideas, we can easily become blinded from seeing smaller, otherwise 'good' and 'valuable' solutions.

Like the story I heard of an employee in the mailroom who noticed several packages being couriered to the same address. He checked into it, compiled them into one package with instructions on distribution at the receiving end. His 'small' change in process saved his company tens of thousands of dollars each year.

While not as flashy or showy, these smaller insights and innovative ideas often represent very workable and profitable options. Some can even lay the foundation for other great ideas or new products and services.

Encourage your team to capture or share their ideas with you, and investigate all of the options contained. Consider that the 'original' idea for the $1 billion dollar a year, Levi Strauss Dockers line came from one of their employees in Argentina (who worked on the docks).

Time to sweat – perspiration activities

- What can you do to fertilize your mind for enhanced brainstorming, or thunder thinking, as I like to call it? *(Thunder thinking™ – when lightning strikes!)*
- What kind of research or mental preparation or 'perspiration' activities will help you and your fellow leaders and professionals?

Suggestions applied successfully by creative thinkers

- Visit authoritative web sites and learn how to use search engines to conduct on-line research
- Challenge your existing assumptions and mindsets. No sacred cows!
- Remember to have fun! We learn best during times of enjoyment.
- Use Google's news alert program to keep you informed on selected areas (other search engines and web based programs will provide this type of material, often on a daily basis.) I have several news topics on leadership, creativity, and innovation and get emails with links to those stories on a daily basis. Primes my pump!
- Read books and magazine articles on the topic you are studying.
- *'Why Didn't I THINK of That?'* might be a good addition to your leadership success library. (Updated 2014) www.Successpublications.ca
- Map out the information you need and potential sources where you might find it. Then go looking!
- Ask open-ended questions to draw out or elicit the most usable and rich information.
- Ask carefully crafted questions of experts in the area of your study. They will often be able to 'kick start' your creativity, give you a heads up, and advance your process to the next level.
- Don't be afraid to ask seemingly stupid questions – there aren't any!
- Learn to apply the four step creative process to fully explore your ideas: preparation, incubation, illumination, and, of course, implementation or taking action on the idea.

 "Creativity can solve almost any problem.
The creative act, the defeat of habit by originality
overcomes everything." George Lois

Harness the power of 'gratitude'

When you are reminded of the 'positive' things – the things that are going right in your life, you get a boost of energy and it helps you remain focused on working more productively. I actually have a list of people and accomplishments I am grateful for in my life and career. I have a 'warm fuzzy' file on my laptop for kudos and acknowledgements from people who have gotten value from something I have done, said, or wrote. When I need them, I simply open it and read! I get inspired again!

From 'KAI-ZEN' to 'I CAN!'
Improvement = Consistent commitment to good change

Kai = *change*   Zen = *good*
When they are used together = *improvement*

Kai-zen came to popularity in North America during the mid 1980's, after becoming an integral part of the Japanese management theory. Western management consultants used it to embrace a wide range of management practices, which were regarded as primarily Japanese. These practices were thought to be the secrets of the strength of Japanese companies in the areas of continual improvement rather than innovation.

According to this theory, the strength of Japanese organizations lay in their attention to process rather than results. They also concentrated the team efforts to continually improve imperfections at each stage of the process. According to them, over the long term, the final result was more reliable, of better quality, more advanced and attractive to clients, and less expensive than Western Management practices.

Its roots however are from an American influence following the 2nd World War. **General Douglas MacArthur** approached several leading US experts to visit Japan to advise them on how to proceed with rebuilding their country and their economy. One expert was **Dr. Edwards Deming (1900-1993).**

He initially came to Japan to conduct a census, but noticed the newly emerging industries were having difficulty. He had been involved in reducing waste in US War manufacturing and drew on that experience to offer his advice. By the 1950's, he was a regular visitor, offering advice to Japanese manufacturers that were having challenges in terms of raw materials, components, and investment; additionally suffering from low morale in the nation and workforce. By the 1970's, many of Japan's leading organizations had embraced Dr. Deming's key points for management. Most are as valid today as they were a half-century ago.

Here are some that relate specifically to the concept called Kai-zen.

- An improved philosophy to effectively deal with change and client needs.
- Constant pursuit of purpose required for improvement of products and services.

- Improving every process for planning, production, and service.
- Instituting or embedding on-going, on the job training for all staff using a variety of methods and ideas.
- Instituting and supporting leadership that is aimed and focused on helping people do a better job. *(Isn't that the true purpose of 21st Century leadership and management?)*
- Breaking down the barriers and boundaries that exist within departments and people. *(GE's CEO, Jack Welsh took this one on personally in his style of management.)*
- Encouraging education for the self-improvement of every member of the organization.
- Top management is committed to improve *'all'* these points, specifically quality and leadership.

Adapting the Kai-zen attitude to our western way of doing business requires a 'major change in corporate culture' – creating a corporate culture that:

- Admits openly and honestly there are problems and challenges.
- Encourages a positive, collaborative, consultative attitude to solving or overcoming them.
- Actively 'devolves' responsibility to the most appropriate or effective level. The person who is in the best position to deal with the challenge or problem needs to have the time, the tools, and the authority to do so.
- Promotes continuous skills-based training and development of attitudes.

Traditionally, the Japanese approach has embedded Kai-zen in its hierarchical structural, although it gives substantially more responsibilities within certain fixed boundaries.

The key features of this management approach and focus are:

- Attention to process, rather than results: Analyze every part of the process down to the smallest detail, with a view to improving them. Looks at how employee's actions, equipment, and materials can be improved.
- Cross-functional management: Management team has an expanded focus to help improve the process and the skills of the people outside the typical western turf wars.
- Use of quality circles; and other tools to support their commitment to continuous improvement.

A range of tools have been developed, along the KAI-ZEN line, to assist companies to make tangible improvements:

- **Quality Control Circles**: groups of people whose primary focus and purpose is to continually improve quality.
- **Process-oriented management**: more attention focused on the 'how' (the process) rather than the 'what' (the task).
- **Visible management**: top executives are being seen, 'walking the job' (management by walking around) and being available to 'see' and consult on each stage of the process.
- **Cross-functional management**: working across functional divides and typical barriers or boundaries, to provide more unity, sense of team, and a wider vision that engages and involves everyone.
- **Just-in-time management**: control of stock and other materials and components to avoid unnecessary expenditures.
- **PDCA**: a process of **P**lan, **D**o, **C**heck, **A**ct to assist in solving challenges.
- **Statistical process control**: enable each machine operator or member of a team to control and measure quality at each stage of the process.

In the Japanese approach to Kai-zen, all of these tools are used in a holistic manner. Contrast this to the current western approach where some of these tools are individually introduced as the 'answer' to every problem or challenge, without consideration of the context within which they were designed to work effectively.

Some perceived benefits of this Kai-zen type of approach:
- Can lead to a reduction of 'wasted' time and resources
- Can increase productivity
- Relatively easy to introduce – requires no major capital investment
- Can lower the break-even point
- Enables organizations to react quickly to market changes
- Appropriate for fast and slow economies as well as growing or mature markets

However, we face some **challenges of introducing Kai-zen** into the western management mind-set.

- **It can be difficult to achieve Kai-zen in practice**, as it requires a complete or major change in attitude and culture. It needs the energy and commitment of all employees. It also requires a substantive investment of time by leaders and their respective teams.

- **It can be difficult to maintain enthusiasm** for several reasons: some see Kai-zen as a threat to their jobs; poor ideas tend to be put forward along with good ideas, which can at times be de-motivating; by implication, there is never complete satisfaction.
- **Continuous improvement is not sufficient or a stand-alone approach in itself.** Major innovation is still needed. There is a danger of becoming 'evolutionary' in focus to the exclusion of being 'revolutionary' or innovation sensitive.

In this turbulent, global economy, organizations need to look seriously at any and all methods, tools, techniques, and training processes that might help in this quest for growth. Kai-zen's step-by-step approach is in direct contrast to the great leaps forward many organizations experience via the innovation avenue.

It is almost as though we need to develop a 'bi-focal' approach and viewpoint, which is one that encompasses steady, continuous improvement of current processes, products, and services, while looking for and encouraging creativity and innovation in moving the organization to the next level. (I do this in the development of my various training programs and publications.)

Kai-zen should free up time for senior managers to think about the long-term future of the organization, look for new opportunities, and move to a concentration on 'strategic' issues. Kai-zen can support improvement of 'existing' activities; but it will not provide the impetus for the innovation process, which often provides our great leaps forward. A balanced approach is called for here.

- It is the role of 'strategic' leadership to take responsibility for the implementation of an effective corporate mission (purpose or soul), reward, and the organizational structure.
- It is the responsibility of 'tactical and strategic' managers to model and practice sound leadership, to promote good teamwork, and to work to ensure everyone understands their roles and the process itself.
- It is the responsibility of 'everyone' in the organization (from front-line to senior management), to measure themselves and their teams; to identify in quantifiable, measurable terms, areas for improvement; and to generate ideas to change practice and procedures. Then, continue measurement to ensure this improvement has been achieved, recorded, and celebrated.
- Each time it is measured, it can be analyzed and a new standard achieved or set and measured. This becomes the cycle of continual improvement. (I CAN!)

Here is a typical or **suggested 'cycle' or process**:

- generate ideas
- evaluate ideas
- decide on action
- plan implementation
- design measurement system
- **take action**
- set new standard
- measure
- analyze
- define problem/desired state
- identify areas for improvement
- generate ideas

Everyone on your team needs to be 'totally' committed to this cycle of continuous improvement. Each team member must be given the knowledge, skills, and tools to be able to participate fully and enthusiastically. They need to participate, not only within their own respective teams; but also across the organization as a whole, as a part of a cross-functional team.

For this to become a reality, work must be undertaken to reinforce or build the confidence within your staff to take on greater responsibility, or make decisions for themselves.

This is an underlying foundation to the work we did in writing and creating *'The Brick Way – It's about ALL of us'* for a major Canadian Retailer. We wanted to send and support the message of each member of their 7000 team taking additional responsibilities and personal leadership over their respective roles. We wanted to instill a new culture and work to create a *'Company of Leaders'*.

This reinforcement is crucial to Kai-Zen's success. In addition to specific skills training and use of tools and knowledge, it is important for us to work on the 'climate for change'; to ensure it is embedded in our corporate culture.

The core values within a Kai-zen based approach to which each of us can aspire are:

- Trust and respect for every member of the team across the organization, not just his or her own team. (Not just their department, their own specialization, expertise, or level.)
- Each individual on a team should be able to openly admit any mistakes or failings they've made or exist in their role and work on doing a better job the next time. Responsibility is an individual commitment. Progress is impossible without the ability to admit, learn from, and move forward from mistakes.

A few years back, I listened to '*A Power Talk*' CD from **Tony Robbins**, in which he shared his concept of CANI (Constant and Never Ending Improvement) for use in our day-to-day lives and roles as leaders. He was quite passionate about his commitment to this concept and for its implementation in our daily lives. He advocated a commitment to constant and never ending improvement.

I'd like to take a 'robbins-esque' approach, and challenge each of you to take a moment to digest what we've discussed about this transplanted US – filtered through Japan approach to management, as a part of your leadership role. I reworded it to a more positive **'I CAN'** acronym. **Improvement is continual and never ending.**

If you and your team are going to be successful in taking your organization to the next level of growth, each of you will need to get a firm foundation and focus on the process of Kai-zen style continual improvement. This is in addition to your personal leadership in applied innovation or Ideas At Work! - as they apply to your changing roles and the teams you seek to lead.

My challenge for each of you: Develop an 'I CAN!' approach and attitude to your leadership and team management, and to equip and inspire those you would seek to lead. 'Improvement is continual and never ending' and it starts with me!'

You can use this 'I CAN' Kai-Zen based focus in your quest to free up time that you choose to reinvest in the lives and skills of those you lead.
Enjoy the journey! In the 'Kai-zen' or 'I CAN!' world, the journey is the goal and provides the sense of achievement and satisfaction. It really works for top performing leaders and their teams as they remain committed to continual improvement in how they leverage their time and enhance their productivity.

The 21st Century version of the 3 R's

The 3 R's used to be: Reading, writing, and 'rithmetic. We need to redefine them to deal with the complex challenges we face today. Most innovations are not entirely new; in fact, many represent new combinations or modifications of current existing services, products, technologies, or materials.

I've done this with my writing and programs by drawing from previous programs or writing in the creation of something more adapted or relevant to my audiences. In fact, we drew from some of our other publications, class notes, surveys, and resources in this revamped edition of *'Running TOO Fast?'*

Not re-inventing the wheel each time, but taking it a step up in the development of its use and scope is a good way to 'leverage your time' and expertise. Fortunately, computers, word processing, visual outlining, or diagramming programs make it easier to gather, analyze, and manipulate information fragments into new combinations or versions for use.

This allows you to apply **these 21st Century 3 R's in your creative process**.

- **Research**, retrieve, and record information.
- **Review** and revise the information you gather.
- **Recombine** or re-use ideas – make new associations between the idea fragments of information you've gathered.

A few tips to help facilitate your creative process

With the proper preparation, any one of your team members can experience an 'ah-ha' moment. Properly applied, each team member can accomplish it. It takes training, but it is not something only an Einstein would be able to do.

- Know where to look for information. Love learning – become a sponge for information on your topic or field of study.

- Develop the skill of asking incisive, well thought-out, open-ended questions that draw out the information, the insights, and the wisdom of those you approach.

- Experiment with mind mapping or other right brain stimulation tools to map out your assumptions, questions, insights, concerns, and needs for more information.

- During the interim (time delay or pause) between your 'Thunder-thinking'™ and specific brainstorming sessions, remain open for additional insights. Be a mental sponge starting with your industry or profession and flowing outward, upward, into cross-functional disciplines, business, social, or other areas. The insight you seek may not be found in the place you live or work, but it is out there.

- Cultivate an 'insight-outlook'. Be open to consider information, insights, trends, and other data mined from multiple perspectives and personal experience. Work to identify and understand the inferences, underlying trends or connections they may contain and how they might pertain or impact what you are working on in your study.

 "Do not be squeamish about your actions.
All life is an experiment."
Ralph Waldo Emerson

Tap into the power of your health

Investing time to ensure you are in good health is important to successfully tackle the demands and pressures in this increasingly hectic world. Keeping your energy levels and mental well being on track is a worthy investment.

- **Manage your stress and anxiety** by doing some form of exercise: for example, run, swim, ride, ski, jog, tennis, or dance.
- **Create a healthy diet** that gives you the energy needed to succeed.
- **Get annual check-ups** – enlist your doctor as a part of your team.
- **Drink water** – keep your body and your brain hydrated. Water also helps flush toxins and other 'junk' out of your system.
- **Sleep is a weapon** – sleep more; sleep better so you have the energy to get more done. Don't watch the news before bedtime.
- **Take naps when your energy is low**. Learn from successful people like Einstein who understood the value of listening to his body and allowing time to recharge.
- **Plan in advance to reduce stress**. For example, lay out your clothes the night before so you don't have to rush in the morning.

Confidence about Credibility

"No one gets taken seriously in this world unless he or she has credibility. Not credibility about brilliant ideas or heroic deeds, but credibility about daily habits and performance." Anonymous

These are four crucial 'Credibility Habits' for top performing business leaders and their teams.

Your clients, leaders, colleagues, and co-workers want to be able to trust and rely on you to do what you say you'll do – when you say you'll do it. This is how you create and enhance mutually beneficial relationships.

A successful and sustainable leadership or business career is built on established credibility

A quick refresher on business etiquette

Four basic ways in which we establish and build on our credibility

- How would you rate yourself and your co-workers or staff in these areas?
- Are there areas in which you see improvement needed at your organization or in your personal dealings?

Showing up on time

Time is the most valuable commodity we have. It is precious in that it is finite and cannot be banked or saved – it must be invested or used wisely. This can make or break your reputation and business. Ever been waiting for someone to show up only to have them rush in spouting excuses? How did that make you feel?

When you 'devalue' my time – you devalue me – and yourself!

Show me that I can count on you to be there when you say and people will begin to trust you and either follow you or deal with you for a long time. I make a point of being early whenever possible. Less stress and if something happens I am usually still able to make it on time.

Doing what you say

Following through and actually doing what you say is very rare. All too often, based on experience, we expect to be disillusioned, to be lied to, and to be disappointed. When we aren't, we are pleasantly surprised and your credibility soars with us.

Under promise and over deliver! This works with leading by example, big time! It works even better for professional people who are focused on helping their clients get what they need.

Finishing what you start

What a nice surprise when we discover that you actually finish what you start. What a difference this makes in the corporate field. Doing this will dramatically set you apart from your competition.

Resolve to start and complete what you commit to doing if you would build a successful business or career. Invest your time wisely and complete on time.

This one will do wonders for your own belief in 'you'. When you finish what you start, you build into your subconscious a belief system that will actively support you when you set a goal. When you have a history of un-finished projects, goals, or commitments your subconscious says, 'Sure you will!' and will not actively reinforce your achievements. Think about it!

Saying please and thank you

Common courtesy is not that common. Showing appreciation for people and their willingness to pursue dealing with you or buying from your firm. As individuals, we are too often treated with a lack of civility and respect. Being courteous and demonstrative in our appreciation will serve you well and win loyalty. This is an underused skill in relation to working with our teams.

These simple habits may seem self-evident, but the failure to observe them is probably the biggest cause of credibility loss in our relationships with others; clients and staff alike. The sad part is this takes very little time and can make such a big difference. When was the last time someone made you feel special and appreciated?

In an increasingly competitive global economy our clients want to feel special and they want to be able to trust you. Our staff want the same things. More so, with increasing competition on a global scale, credibility is a survival and business-building tool.

Walk your talk and see the results

- In light of your reflection of the above factors, how would you change what you're doing now to ensure they get that opportunity?
- Are there areas you need to polish a bit and perhaps consciously focus on doing more often?

Allowing your clients, leaders, colleagues, and co-workers to see for themselves your actions speaking in support of your words is a *foundation for success* in any endeavour.

Often, a promising career has been derailed, not from lack of knowledge, but from lack on one or more of these essential credibility traits. Build your career on some 'solid' foundations for long-term success!

 "A man who dares to waste one hour of life has not discovered the value of life."
Charles Darwin

Harness the power of your schedule

Successful people create routines and schedules that allow them to focus their energies on the most important activities needed. They know the value of applied habit and routine as proven by champions in every field. They work to streamline their schedules and minimize those activities that distract them. They plan for success and build strong success habits.

- **Prioritize one item per day.** Focus on your highest value or one of your vital few activities that moves you forward.
- **Use a 'Focused Five' approach as you plan your work week.**
- **Schedule email and return phone calls.** Group them.
- **No meetings unless they are decisive.** Guard your time!
- **Set a daily routine.** Build success habits that allow you to win.
- **Manage the mornings.** Do your vital few activities first thing.
- **Do something easy first – to kick start your day.** Success to start.
- **Never schedule more than 50% of your day.** Life happens in the midst of our schedule, so plan for it.
- **Build in flex time to allow for 'interruptions'.** Schedule more time than you think something will take. I suggest 125% as a general rule.

How much are you 'really' working?

If I asked how many of you were really busy, I know I'd get close to 90% saying yes. If I asked how many were 'working' more than 50 hours a week, the answer might be 70% or more.

The critical question is, **"How many of you feel like you've effectively used your time during the last week?"** The answers here would be lower; less than 50% of respondents in my sessions thought they were using their time effectively. That lower response is one of the reasons for sharing these ideas.

The second reason was the knowledge that the best way to 'learn' something was to 'teach' it. And, I really wanted to 'learn'! With my overloaded schedule and commitments, I was motivated to 'learn'. I wanted then, and still do, my freedom and control of my life and time.

One of the 'freedom' tools developed, in addition to my daily schedule, was the use of a simple log-book. I'd suggest creating one for your personal use. A friend who works as an accountant, told me she keeps something like this close at hand to track her 'billable' hours and found it helpful. I found it helped me track my 'productive' hours invested in my business.

It was invaluable as a periodic checkup on how I 'actually' use my time. A check on how much 'real work' was accomplished each day. A check up on how much time was spent with the important people in my life. A check up on how available hours are allocated to accomplishing life goals I've set.

Management expert, **Peter Drucker** was a strong advocate of this idea. Before planning on how one wishes to spend their time, he recommended you first need to know 'where' you are spending it. Made sense to me! This can be a sobering form, if you approach it openly and honestly. It will help you get a real grip on 'your' time wasters and help improve your overall effectiveness in managing your life and your time. It can be an indicator of misplaced values and a misguided sense of purpose.

Luci Swindoll wrote, *"Purpose or mission is determined by the development of values, balance, ethics, humor, morality, and sensitivities. It manifests itself in the way we look at life."*

The best method I've found is to simply go about your regular day, with the exception of making notes on the various activities you engage in during that day. For example:

- meetings
- conversations
- phone calls to clients
- pricing
- travel
- coffee and snack breaks
- drop in visitors
- sleeping
- child care
- cooking
- day dreaming
- correspondence
- internet
- dealing with client problems
- personal errands
- TV
- entertainment
- talking with your spouse, or special someone
- spiritual time
- socializing
- phone calls
- client interviews
- job site
- commuting
- washroom activities
- eating
- housework
- shopping
- water cooler conferences
- research
- reading the paper
- reading work related materials
- community work
- family time
- sports
- love making
- time with your kids
- other activities

I think you get the idea? On any given day we are involved in a host of activities, the above list covering only some of them from experience. Many of you will have additions to this list.

Deliberately take a minute 'every half hour' and jot down what you did during that time. Don't stop to analyze it or try to artificially make it look good by justifying any action. At this point, simply record your use of time in 5, 10, or 15-minute increments. From experience, the half-hour record works better than every 15 minutes. Consider doing this for 3 to 5 days until you get the hang of it. Don't worry if you miss a few points. You are the only one who sees this check-in sheet.

At the end of your 'test' period, take your sheets and be brutally honest when looking at them. Actually total the activities by category. For example, REAL WORK, family time, personal, filler time, wasted time, etc. I'm sure you'll see a trend appearing in how you really use your time and where you may be a bit less effective than you want to be.

If you are aware of how you 'presently' use time, you will be better equipped to make the changes to make better use of it in the future.

You'll have the opportunity to reflect and refine how you value your time and the activities in which you invest it. Do this periodically as a check up on how well you are now using your time, and to give you a sense of the areas where you still 'need' a little work!

Someone close to me told me, *"Show me how you spend your time and I'll know your values in life!"* What will your daily schedule - time log reveal about your choices in life? And once you've seen it, what will you do with the information?

You can break down or group the activities as needed for your own research. It doesn't have to be pretty, just accessible and easy to use. This is for your awareness only. Good Luck!

We've included a couple of examples on the following pages. We invite you to visit our website to download blank forms for your personal use. We have also added additional resources for your use in regaining your freedom. Visit: **www.SuccessPublications.ca/TimeTools.htm**

 "People spend and excessive amount of time conjugating three verbs: 'To Want', 'To Have', and 'To Do'. We had forgotten that 'To Be' is the source and fount of life."
Unknown

In search of a 'balanced' life

My generous friend and co-author **Brian Tracy,** talks about balancing work and home. "You don't have to be a superman or superwoman to properly balance the demands of your work and the needs of your family. You must, however, be more thoughtful, be a better planner, use your time more effectively, and continually think of ways to enhance the quality of your life in both areas."

DAILY SCHEDULE FOR: _____ **Date:** _____

Goals: (1) _____ (2)_____
(3) _____ (4) _____

Time	Meetings	Phone	Work	Travel	Personal	Reading	Clients
8:00							
8:30							
9:00							
9:30							
10:00							
10:30							
11:00							
11:30							
Noon							
12:30							
1:00							
1:30							
2:00							
2:30							
3:00							
3:30							
4:00							
4:30							
5:00							
Totals							

Please notice the addition of your daily goals at the top of this sample daily schedule. My belief is looking at your goals every 30 minutes will help to embed them in your subconscious. That alone, will be an invaluable asset to your quest to get free once you know where you presently spend your time.

This example is a business day based chart. You might want to adapt yours to meet your specific needs, especially if you work from home or a small office in your home as many of us do. Getting to know how you presently spend your time is the best foundation for doing better. You might prefer using the example on the next page. Or do them both to give you a snapshot of how you currently spend your time.

The idea here is to get an idea on how you use your time now, so you can decide how you want invest it or leverage it for better effectiveness in the future.

Visit: **www.SuccessPublications.ca /TimeTools.htm** for this form and other downloadable forms and blanks, along with other bonus resources designed to help you in your quest to get free.

Date: _____   **My Time Log Template:** _____

Goals: (1) _____ (2) _____

(3) _____ (4) _____

TIME	ACTION/ ACTIVITY	PRIORITY 1 = Important/Urgent 2 = Important/ Non Urgent 3 = Urgent/Not Important 4 = Routine	COMMENTS Delegate to: _____ Teach _____ to do it Next time say 'No' Estimate/consolidate/cut

Here is another version of a daily time log. Again, keep your goals in mind and go back and analyze the activity in relation to its importance. Make comments about the activity so you might know what to do next time. Again, these different formats are simply examples of what you could create and use in your quest to see where you spend your time and to better plan where you will more productively plan it in the future.

Visit www. SuccessPublications.ca /TimeTools.htm for a downloadable copy of this form; along with additional surveys, logs and time tools and special bonus surprises for our readers.

How to use the information from your Daily Schedule Time-log or other check-up forms

Once you've done some research as to how you invest your time, you can move ahead to regaining control and to better leveraging your time. The secret is to carve out some 'undisturbed time' to analyse and reflect on what you've learned from logging your time use. Take along your personal and professional goals, the time logs, and some blank paper and retire to a place where you will not be disturbed.

After carefully considering the trends you discover, ask yourself these questions:

- How did I waste my time? What can I do to prevent or minimize time waste in the future?
- How did I waste other people's time? Be honest here! It is in learning to respect the time of others that we learn to respect and demand respect ourselves.
- How can I prevent this from happening in the future?
- Who or what was the biggest distraction or waster of my time? How will I handle them or that?
- What activities am I now doing that can be reduced, delegated, or eliminated? How and when will I accomplish these changes?
- What did other people do that wasted my time? What can I do to prevent or minimize these types of time wasters? How will I implement these roadblocks to time wasting?
- What did I do today that was urgent, but in retrospect - not important? How will I keep my focus and get the important things done in the future?
- Am I really spending or investing my time pursuing those things I value and feel are important in my life? If not, why not? How will I change my schedule to do this?
- Did I spend time with the people who matter to me; the ones who are important in my life? If not, why not? How will I create time to invest in them in the future?

Habits are hard to break. **Samuel Johnson** once wrote, *"The chains of habits are too weak to be felt until they are too strong to be broken."*

Using the daily schedule/log as a tool to periodically revisit your progress will give you a better chance to break those chains or form some new strong ones that will help you free up you live for the important people and priorities in your life.

One of the best aids to overcoming time-wasting habits is to learn how to effectively schedule your time. Most of us simply use our schedule as a glorified TO DO list. I still do on occasion. If you use it more effectively, integrate your personal and professional activities into a single book. You will find your effectiveness soaring. Find the type of schedule that works for you and USE IT!

 "Just because you have the skills, doesn't mean you have the time." **Bob 'Idea Man' Hooey © 1991**

I finally figured this out and realized I was taking great learning opportunities away from other people by jumping in 'simply' because I had the experience or the expertise. When I started focusing on helping people grow and on learning to effectively delegate my responsibilities, I saw white space in my planner and breathing space in my life. I also saw others start to bloom as they took personal leadership and responsibility for their roles. A double win!

Note: I am so grateful to my amazing friend **Harold Taylor**, CSP, HoF for his leadership in this critical area. I have learned so much from his generosity and wisdom. I am grateful for him licensing me to use some of his insightful materials in my own client work. This has allowed me to better serve my audiences and readers over the years. He has long been a leader in this field and has now successfully moved into semi-retirement. I'm working to follow his lead there too.

I still use his *Taylor Planner - time management system* after all these years, as it works well for me. I find it is a valued collection of my notes, contacts, ideas, schedules, and observations. I even add to it after an event to ensure I record anything of value. These day timers are part of my life story over the past dozen or so years. I keep them as references to tap into as I move into a new year. They allow me to remember my past dreams, goals, and activities. Nice to go back and reflect.

Visit his website to buy some of his brilliant materials to help you in your quest to get free and become more productive both personally and professionally. www.taylorintime.com Tell them, Bob Hooey sent you.

Building blocks help make your life more effective

I have found these ideas to be helpful. Quite simply, I have found it simple to allocate or schedule specific blocks of time in my daytimer for my various activities and priorities. I admit, it doesn't always work as planned; but overall my productivity has improved.

- **Block out time to plan.** This is the real freedom secret. Take time to pre-plan your day, your week, your month, and even your year. This simple task can take as little as five minutes and yet it can save you hours.

Remember - **Plan Monthly, Schedule Weekly, and Live/LEAD Daily.**

- **Block out committed time.** Here, you block out time you have little control over, such as doctor's appointments, business or community based meetings, out-of-town trips, classes or workshops, association meetings, work, and related activities. You may find it a bit sobering to see how little of your time is really yours at present. Don't get frustrated, get free! Resolve to make changes and start freeing up this time. Blocking it out in your time management aid will also help you stop over committing as you can see at a glance how committed you are now!

- **Block out and outline deadlines and checkpoints.** When you take on a project and it has a real deadline, mark it in your time management system. Then work backwards to build in checkpoints on the various parts of the project and the time deadlines they require to be done. For example, if it takes two weeks to typeset, proof, and print a report and it has to be in by June 1st, you know it has to be written and edited before May 15th. Build in some flexibility and work ahead of the concrete deadlines so you're not caught red faced when something goes wrong or someone lets you down. Be realistic in the estimation of time needed for the component parts of your project. Work back from the deadline and block out specific times to work on the various parts. If you do this, you will find yourself less likely to say 'Yes' when you don't have the time.

81

- **Design in flexibility to handle the surprises in life**. Expect the unexpected, someone once told me! Design in breathing room! It's nice to run on a tight time schedule, but realistically, unless we design in some flex time, we schedule to frustrate ourselves. One rule of thumb is to estimate the time it will take for an activity and multiply by 1.25 and use that figure. Another rule of thumb is only schedule up to 50% of your time. This will leave chunks available for the inevitable surprises and sometimes-pleasant events that happen in our daily lives. It will keep the pressure and stress of unfulfilled schedules from ruining your day. Schedules are designed to help us use our time more effectively - to free time for the important people and priorities in our lives!

TIME TIP: I use only 'one' central planner to block out all my time. I use other ones, such as my Outlook calendar, or on my Smart Phone calendar as reminders of specific activities.

- **Block out time for your spouse and family.** This is a very important point as it impacts you where you live and influences your life in ways too numerous to discuss here. My friend, TIME Guru **Harold Taylor** even suggested scheduling a date with your spouse in INK. He said the resulting response to his wife experiencing her importance to him, made a distinctive difference in the quality of his life. Too often, we value others and clients more than our spouse and family. We also pay a price that is way too dear! My wife, **Irene**, and I maintain a 2 month calendar at the top of the stairs; she has her office downstairs and mine is upstairs. We each indicate committed time for our individual activities. We also block out time for us!

- **Block out time for spiritual and/or reflection time.** Someone told me once that we are a spiritual being having a physical experience. I do know we have a mental, physical, and spiritual balance that takes work and time. What ever your personal belief system, you will experience numerous benefits when you take time to commune, reflect, and talk with your maker; or at least reflect on your life. Try it, it works!

- **Block out time for recreation and diversion.** *"All work and no play makes Jack a dull boy - and Jill a wealthy widow,"* writes **Evan Esar**. If you want to be creative and effective in your career, if you want to succeed in life - take a break and have some fun! It is only when you slow down that you have a chance for your body to catch up with your mind and you can return to work rejuvenated and refreshed. Everyone has his or her own schedule. I take a few days every quarter and find it works wonders for my soul and body, to say nothing of what it does for my mind.

- My very productive friend, **Wayne Cotton** even suggests blocking out vacation and break times as a priority. He schedules them first. I like that!

- **Block out time for personal research and study.** My late NSA colleague, Charley 'Tremendous' Jones said, *"Except for the books you read, the places you go, and the people you meet, you will be exactly the same 5 years from now!"* What a scary thought! I want to be better than I am now, having more fun, and leading a more fulfilled life. Take a few minutes and block out time to study, read, and research areas that interest you. Note: I said areas that interest you, **not** just work reading related to your present career. Often, ideas from diverse sources will stimulate your mind and you will bring valuable insights to your present career.

How are you allocating your time? It takes so little to make a BIG difference! Over the years I have allowed myself to reach out to people as I travel and go through my normal work day. I make it a point to schedule less so I actually have a few moments to stop and talk or better yet, simply listen. That is my gift to those I lead!

 "The greatest disease is not TB or leprosy; it is being unwanted, unloved, and uncared for. We can cure physical diseases with medicine, but the only cure for loneliness, despair and hopelessness is love. There are many in the world who are dying for a piece of bread, but there are many more dying for a little love." Mother Teresa

---

Leverage your travel time

I used to spend the greater part of my time on the road, either driving or flying between cities. I have chosen to reduce my travel time to allow me to enjoy time with my wife and in other activities closer to home.

I've worked to minimize my 'waiting' or 'prep' time while on the road. I have (2) fully loaded toiletry kits which makes it simple to pack. I just grab one and go. Similarly, I often pack underwear and socks in zip locks along with shirts. This allows them to be moved for inspection without fuss going through security. This saves time and frustration.

With the advent of advance online check-ins I can print my boarding pass and (when travelling light) go right to the gate. I can also head right to the car rental or shuttle at my destination. We have included more travel time tips later in the book.

How much is your time 'really' worth?

Have you ever taken a moment and thought about what your time is 'really' worth? Have you ever calculated your earning capacity (in dollars and cents) on an hourly basis? It can be a great exercise in determining your worth, relative value, and earning contribution. It can also tell you how much each minute or hour you allow to be wasted is really costing you.

Let's figure out a typical time/value calculation. Using a typical year with 2 vacation weeks and 10 paid holidays leaves us with only 240 work days in which to earn our living. Assuming an average 8-hour workday this gives us 1920 potential work hours in a year.

On the surface we'd simply take our Gross Pay and divide by the hours, e.g. $50,000/year would give us an average hourly rate of $26.04 per hour. So in this instance each 15-minute block of wasted time would be costing you $6.51. Work it out for your salary, commissions, or earnings level.

Let's take this a bit further, shall we? In all honesty, would you say that you are able to get 8 productive hours in each 8-hour day? My guess, of course not! Honest feedback from quite a few of our North American audience members puts the 'true number' somewhere closer to a generous 60% effectiveness on any given day. I know some of you are saying, *"I only wish I had a 60% rate."* If that is true, then we really have only 1152 work hours in which to make our money. In the example above, each hour would now be worth $43.04 and each 15-minute block costing us $10.85.

Most of us would not 'deliberately' waste a full day, but often let 15 minute segments slip away without notice or regret. This is one of the foundation points of success as a leader. Take back your time and choose to invest it in your growth and in that of your team.

Here are some rough comparisons for different dollar earning levels

Annual Earnings	Hourly rate	60% Effective rate	15 min. block
50,000/year	$26.04	$43.40	$10.85
100,000/year	$52.08	$86.80	$21.70
200,000/year	$104.16	$173.60	$43.40

Very interesting figures aren't they? If you remain aware of what your time is 'really' worth it will help you keep an eye on the time wasters that creep into your life. Not that I put a monetary price on everything in my life; but it is good to know what my 'investment or contribution' is really worth. I invoice my no-fee clients showing the real value of what I just 'gave' them. This is as much for me as them to remind me of the value I provide.

After my dad died, I spent quite a lot of time with my mom before she too passed away. It was probably the best return for my time investment I've ever made – priceless! I'd do it again in a heartbeat if I could.

Our objective here is not to focus on the money, but to allow it (money) to visibly remind you how 'valuable' your time really is as a leader or top level working professional.

When working with executives and their teams on liberating time, we challenge them to focus on liberating (saving) 5 to 15 minute blocks of time from their over-committed schedules. Their objective is creating at least one or more 15 minute block a day. Those 15 minute 'choices' (segments) can be invaluable when focused or re-invested on your more important priorities, one of which would be 'working' with your teams.

Based on an improved age span of 85 years, we have ONLY 31,046 days to LIVE! Roughly 745,000 hours in which to live out our dreams, accomplish our life goals, and make an impact on our world and those with whom we share it. My bet many of you reading this are at least a quarter of the way down your path. Time is moving quickly and we have critical choices to make. According to Goethe, *"One always has enough time, provided one spends it well."*

What difference would that make if you were able to spend it better?

Time savings - what is it 'really' costing you?

Have you ever calculated some of the 'decisions' you make in your life in relation to the time they 'cost' you and the real cost of that time? For example where you live, what activities you spend your time in, where you volunteer.

For example, let's discuss where you live in relation to where you work. There is a growing trend of people living a good distance away from where they work. Economically it would seem to be a good trade off - on the surface. But there are costs involved, monetary and non-monetary, that should be considered in deciding if this trade off is worth it for you.

Non-monetary costs would encompass things like reduced time with family and spouse, increased commute time, increased stress, wear and tear mentally, increased auto expenses, missing activities and important events with family, and increased chance of accident or injury. Others may come to mind.

Let's look at the commute time, shall we?

If you commute over 30 minutes each day to work and back there is a 'real cost' in your time and the impact on your life. 30 minutes each way works out to 240 hours per year which effectively a full six weeks on your work schedule. If your commute is 60 minutes each way, which is 12 weeks or a full 3 months spent just sitting in your vehicle or in the transit system.

Your time allotment can be even more expensive than the operations and replacement cost of the vehicle itself. Take a look and factor in your real and effective numbers. Take a moment and calculate what it is costing you to have this commute in your work week. Check your effective hourly rate on the previous page - $50,000 for this example.

Commute time _____ x effective hourly rate _____ = _____

Eg.   **240 hours   x   43.40   = $10,416/year**

 Using the $50,000 per year figures (above) shows my commute is costing me 21% of my salary. WOW!

How much do you have to make to clear and extra 21%? Interesting question and one not previously considered. I do now when charging for my programs, after factoring in the actual presentation time, travel time, on-site time, and preparation time. My clients are getting a bargain at only $_____. ☺ Plus, I'm thinking of raising it a bit this year!

The one commodity we have to trade for an income, which is not replaceable, is our time. Use it and sell it wisely. Time is money, but more importantly it is life. LIVE IT WELL!

 "To accomplish great things,
we must not only act but also dream,
not only plan but also believe."
Anatole France

Identifying and eliminating your time wasters

Over the years, we've asked our audiences about their time challenges and been able to identify their **25 biggest time wasters.**

Here they are!

1. Telephone interruptions
2. Failure to plan
3. **Attempting TOO much**
4. Drop-in visitors
5. Socializing and daydreaming
6. Ineffective delegation
7. Travel (commuting)
8. Lack of self-discipline
9. **Inability to say NO!**
10. Procrastination – 'busy' work
11. Family concerns
12. Paper work (where is the paperless office they promised me?)
13. Leaving tasks unfinished
14. Not enough staff or personnel
15. Meetings (unnecessary or unproductive)
16. Confused responsibility (I thought 'you' were going to do _____?)
17. Poor verbal and written communication skills
18. Inadequate controls, feedback, or progress reports
19. Inaccurate or incomplete information
20. Personal and corporate disorganization
21. Email, texts, etc. (great if targeted and used appropriately)
22. Management by CRISIS!
23. Cell phones, i-pads, and tablets (they can be great if used properly)
24. Television
25. Surfing the Internet, Facebook, Twitter, etc. (ok, I get caught up on it too!) www.ideaman.net

You may have some of your own time wasters not on this list. In fact, I can name well over 150. Time wasters take away from your high priority time as an innovative, effective leader or professional.

Take a moment to honestly appraise your life and personal leadership activities. Our audiences and leadership clients across North America have helped us come up with some novel approaches to help combat them.

Go through the time wasters on your list.

- Check off the time wasters you recognize (and remember the people who employ them against you) as draining your schedule and energy.
- Identify the major ones that hurt your ability to successfully handle your leadership role.
- Decide to work on each one until you've eliminated or at least tamed it. Then move on to work on others.

Successful life and time management is a journey not a destination. As in any journey, the starting point is just as important as the destination.

One tip: don't try to deal with them all at once. Select the most important ones and work on them until you've beaten them. Then confidently tackle the next ones on your list. It may take some time, but it is so worth it.

Cherish Today!

"Yesterday is but a dream, tomorrow a vision of hope.
Look to this day, for it is life. I cannot change yesterday.
I can only make the most of today, and look with hope toward tomorrow!" Anon

As we discuss some of these time wasters in more detail, new ideas may pop into your mind. Write them down and share them with your friends. Brainstorm real solutions to real problems... then commit immediately to put those ideas into action!

 "Few will have the greatness to bend history itself, but each of us can work to change a small portion of events. It is from numerous acts of courage and belief that human history is shaped."
Robert Fitzgerald Kennedy

Dealing with disorganization

A disorganized or cluttered workspace can cause time delays in searching for items or redoing them because they are lost. Resolve to leave your workspace clean for the next morning with your planning list for the next say right on top. That way you can start your day with energy and focus!

Working from our complied list of the top **25 Time Wasters**, I personally identified my top five time wasters. I began tackling them and, have made significant progress in overcoming their impact on my life and time. I've expanded the group, and am now working on some new challenges. I share them for your consideration and encouragement. Like me, you may find some of them a challenge. I trust these lessons, learned the hard way, may be a guide in your own quest for freedom.

- **Attempting Too Much At Once.** This is one of my biggest ongoing challenges. I have many varied areas of interest in my business and personal life. I have learned to 'BUDGET' my time (like MONEY... because it is!); to allocate specific amounts of time for special projects, research and planning, fun times, appointments, family and friends, community service, Toastmasters, CAPS, NSA, Professional development, Professional Associations, and other commitments.

I started blocking out specific time and scheduling events, projects, and appointments in my Taylor Planner - time management system. I learned this tip from my association with CSP, **Harold Taylor**. It has made a major difference in the past dozen or more years. Scheduling 'all' these areas allows me to see firsthand where I have over-booked and to alert me when I may be getting close to overload or burn out. Again, being honest is the only foundation for long-term freedom.

- **Procrastination.** This used to be a big one, until I 'fell flat on my commitments' a few too many times and had to live down the embarrassment of letting friends and associates down! Now, 'IF' I take on a project (I don't automatically say yes), I have started blocking out chunks of time in my daytimer for research and have estimated and entered 'realistic' deadlines and checkpoints for successfully completing each project. I still occasionally get behind, but find myself less stressed and more focused. It's also more fun to be in control and on schedule.

- **Doing it MYSELF! (Not delegating).** One of the most important decisions I've made in the past 12 or so years was to start setting limits. The second best decision I made was to get my 'I can do anything Ego' under control, and to start asking for help. To my amazement, people are more than responsive when I ask for help.

I find my effectiveness multiplied at a fantastic rate. I've found myself encouraged and supported by sharing the load.

Using the 'freedom' power of effective delegation and collaboration has enabled me to leverage time and allowed me to accomplish more than ever imagined. I found this an extremely valuable tool when serving as President of our CAPS Vancouver Chapter (1999 & 2000), on our CAPS National Board (2000-2002), as President of our CAPS Edmonton Chapter (2012), and as a trustee for our CAPS Foundation (2008-2013). Building and equipping 'productive' teams was worth the time and effort.

1. Ask yourself, **"Is this important?"**
2. Then ask yourself, **"Is it important that I do it, or can someone else do it?"**
3. Does it need to be done **now**?
4. Then, either do it, delegate it, or delay it!

- **Not Saying NO!** Boy has this one been a struggle! All too often I would get so excited with the potential of the opportunity or challenge presented, that I would say 'Yes' without first considering my time commitments and life goals. I have become increasingly 'clearer' on what I want to do with my life and what I need to accomplish my personal and professional goals. This helps me ask the question, *"Will this help me reach one of my life or career goals?"* Then to decide whether to say 'YES' to a request. I have learned the consequence of saying 'yes' too quickly.

Saying 'NO' is still hard; but frequently the alternative has been to say 'NO' to something even more important in my life or career to accommodate the commitment. I have gotten tired of leaving my dreams on the table, as I labor to build someone else's. Someone once wrote, *"If you have inside you a burning 'YES' it is much easier to say NO!"*

- **Personal Disorganization (desk clutter).** Sadly, this is the one that still defeats me on occasion. I am a self-confessed 'pilot'- I have a pile of notes in one corner and a pile of unread magazines or books (that I might need someday) in another. I used to have three desks and sometimes, I could even find the tops of them, but it took work and discipline. But take hope, if I can make headway in this area anyone can. My primary desk still looks like the following cartoon once in awhile, usually when I am in the midst of a writing project. But you can actually see the surface most of the time.

Being able to find something quickly, when you need it, frees up your time for more creative and productive endeavors.

I have designed a specific place for certain information and resources I use regularly, for each of my various involvements. I have a system (still under refinement) for finding the remainder, when needed. This has become even more important as my writing and speaking commitments have increased. As my communications, publishing, and consulting business expands, the plan is to contract out to have the office and accounting work done. This will free me to do what I do and love best!

I have recently re-designed my work area with a large U-shaped desk to accommodate my changing needs. It allows me to creatively work on several different projects in the same time frame, without excess clutter.

I have been cutting back on my 'collecting', and am working harder at only handling paper once. I have even taken to opening my mail 'over' a wastebasket. This has made some major changes in reducing my bulging filing cabinets and in actually seeing my desk surfaces.

A friend told me, *"Each piece of paper on my desk was a decision I hadn't made yet."* Ouch, that one got to me! I have even started periodically purging my files of duplicate material, carbon-dated files ☺, and other areas that I used to think *"I had to keep that one on file".*

Take heart, if you find yourself fighting a few uphill battles to regain control of your time and life. It can be done, but it will require you to concentrate and focus your efforts. As someone once said, *"Inch by inch...life's a pinch, but yard by yard...life can be hard!"* Keep at it - you are definitely worth it! Your family and friends will thank you for the hard work.

My top five time wasters

Take a few moments and look at your earlier list (see page 87). Which five timer wasters are still on your hit list? Hopefully you've taken advantage of doing some brainstorming with your friends and fellow 'freedom fighters'. But you need to act to take advantage of this momentum!

Take a few moments to detail some of these needed actions today. Make specific notes on how you allow or perceive this time waster in your life. Detail specific actions and decisions on how and when you will tackle each of them. This is where you can expand on your earlier thinking about how to deal with them.

1. **Time waster**_____
   ACTION PLAN:

   TIMELINE:

2. **Time Waster**_____
   ACTION PLAN:

   TIMELINE:

3. **Time Waster**_____
   ACTION PLAN:

   TIMELINE:

4. **Time Waster**_____
   ACTION PLAN:

   TIMELINE:

5. **Time Waster** _____
   ACTION PLAN:

   TIMELINE:

Time Waster _____
   ACTION PLAN:

   TIMELINE:

We even gave you a spare, in case you find 6 challenges that just have to be tackled! SMILE! ☺ Identifying your top five time wasters and setting an ACTION PLAN is only half the battle to overcoming their power to minimize your life. The critical and most important part of **Act**ion is ACT.

Schedule a specific time, weekly and daily, to review your action plan; time to make adjustments and to refocus your commitment and energies in finding the freedom you want to do the things you want in your life. This decision to ACT and take control of your life may be one of the most important ones you make this year. Actually moving on that decision will make it a reality!

 "This is the highest wisdom that I own - Freedom and life are earned by those alone who conquer them each day, anew." Goethe

---

Master the power of training

Regaining your freedom means passing along some of those 'non-vital' things to others by effective delegation. Right now I bet you can think of at least three activities you hate that you haven't 'had time' to train someone else to do. Right?

Make the time! Until you do, you will never be free. Invest a day now to train and hand off at least one of these items. This will save you un-countless hours as you move forward and allow you to focus on your 'vital few' activities that actually move you forward.

Converting Filler Time to Foundation Time
How to re-create or liberate 365 hours each year

How would you like to re-create or liberate a minimum of 365 hours each year? That is the equivalent of over 9 weeks of time. Very simple: reclaim, repurpose, or convert a minimum of one hour each day.

One of the more important secrets to regaining control of your time and life is in the conversion of 'filler' or wasted time into 'foundation' or constructive time. Recapturing or re-creating those seemingly 'insignificant' slivers of time (5 - 15 minute chunks) and converting them to more constructive use will make a major difference in your life, leadership, and career advancement.

What I'd like to suggest here are ideas that might help you do just that - capture those 'insignificant' minutes and convert them to useful time. Each of them will help you free up an average of 5 minutes, some substantially more.

Simply incorporate 12 or more of them of them into each day and free up or re-create a minimum of one hour for more useful time.

- Useful time that builds a foundation for success under your dreams and goals.
- Useful time that leads you productively in the direction you've laid out for your future.
- Useful time that previously was thrown away.
- Useful time that allows you to invest time in building and maintaining important relationships.

At home

- Bunch or group your errands.
- Spend 5 minutes each day pre-planning your schedule and activities.
- Trade off with neighbors or friends and share common chores - i.e., kids to school

- Use your time in the shower as pre-planning time to mentally go over your daily schedule and goals.
- Coordinate your business clothing to include suits, shirts, ties, accessories, before bedtime.
- Never make more than one trip if at all possible. Don't backtrack!
- Use a voice mail system on your phone. Some systems assign voice mailboxes for each family member.
- Open your personal mail over a recycling bin.
- Multi-task to combine activities that would normally demand down time or waiting time, for example, cooking and laundry or menu planning.
- Agree on a special family time to discuss and plan family activities.
- Other ideas that may come to mind.

At work

- Spend 5 minutes each day reviewing the current day and pre-planning activities and goals for the next day. Revise your schedule based on 4 P's of Personal Performance principles (see page 34).
- Keep a folder with required reading close at hand for those 'on-hold' times.
- Keep career advancement e-books on your e-reader, computer, and smart phone for creative fill-ins.
- Keep a career enhancement book close at hand for reading breaks.
- Open your mail over your wastebasket or recycle bin.
- Batch your phone calls for specific times each day.
- Return phone calls at specific times each day.
- Check your email only at specific times each day and return emails then.
- Keep your internet use to a minimum and focus on work during work.
- Do any internet surfing, Facebook, Linked in, Twitter posts, etc ONLY on your breaks and resist the temptation to check it during work time.
- Plan what you are going to say before you make a call and have the relevant information or files available for quick reference.
- Multi-task to do more than one job, alternating back and forth between activities instead of just waiting for something to warm up, print, or load.
- Trade off with co-workers to create some 'uninterrupted' planning and creative time.
- Take a few minutes before you leave to de-clutter your desk.
- Take a few minutes before you leave to put out important items for attention first thing in the morning.

While waiting

- Carry a book/e-reader or something to read with you.
- Use your Cell phone to retrieve and return messages.
- Use your smart phone to check your email or make posts to your social media.
- Have a mini-recorder to dictate letters or brainstorm ideas. Use your smart phone for this function.
- Check your various lists and update your action items.
- Check your schedule and revise as needed.
- Brainstorm solutions to challenges you have with your business or personal life.
- Other ideas that may come to mind

While commuting

- Turn your car into a mobile university - listen to MP3s or CDs enroute.
- If using public systems - use a personal MP3 player with ear phones.
- Use your smart phone or GPS to help plan your route.
- Use your smart phone to locate addresses and directions for places you need to find.
- Spend the time revising your schedule and revisiting your priorities and goals.
- Spend the time rehearsing your presentation or sales pitch.
- Other ideas that may come to mind

While traveling

- Pre-select your seat if at all possible. Most airlines will allow you to do this in advance of coming to airport.
- Check in on-line and print your boarding pass. Then go right to security and your gate to save time.
- Pack selected coordinates to allow yourself to take less with you on trips.
- Use a packing list to ensure you have everything you need. Print it and put it in your bag along with your home and local contact information.
- Pack and travel light to avoid long check-ins and waiting for your baggage at your destination.
- Carry selected reading/e-reader to review enroute.
- Load your smart phone with e-books – like this one!

- Take along postcards or send notes and thank you's to selected friends, customers, suppliers and other important people in your life. Take along stamps and drop them in the nearest post box on arrival.
- Take time to review and plan your week in relation to **4P's of Personal Performance.** (see page 34)
- Take the time to specifically plan and revise your planning tool.
- Review magazines and articles that apply to your field of study.
- When driving away from home, use your smart phone or GPS to help plan your route.
- Use your smart phone to locate places you need to find.
- Other ideas that may come to mind

I realize the above are not the 'end all - be all' of how to recapture your time. The exercise here was to show you a few examples of areas where you could reclaim a few minutes here and there to free up time for better or more productive use. You can easily free up an hour a day if you focus!

As you become more focused on recapturing and reclaiming your time, you'll become aware of a multitude of ideas and activities that you can use to convert your filler time into foundation time. Don't despise those 'insignificant' minutes. Just like the 'secret' of compound interest, those minutes if captured and reinvested in your career or future will *multiply* and pay fabulous dividends.

If you come up with some unique or creative ideas would you please email me and share them? If included in subsequent versions of this work, we will credit you and send you a copy of the updated version for your own use. You can email me at: bob@ideaman.net

"Carpe Momento" - seize the moment!

 "Building some air into our schedules pays off. We can create the time to have a leisurely breakfast with our family or take the scenic route to the office and enjoy the ride. We can create daily and weekly variations that will make it possible for us to savor special moments throughout our days, throughout our weeks, and throughout our lives." Elaine St. James

Leveraging technology to get 'more' done

With the continuing explosion and evolution of technology and tools, a few thoughts on how we can use these 'tools' to get more done and enjoy our lives is in order. This advent of changing technology has the potential to assist us in freeing up large chunks of time for other more productive work.

I am by no means an expert on this specific area. However, I'm using these 'tools' and seeing definitive increases in personal productivity. We offer these thoughts for your consideration and application. Our challenge for you is to investigate their value for your situation in freeing up time or leveraging time for increased productivity. My wife, **Irene**, who is our resident techie helped with a few hints on how to leverage technology.

SMART Cell phones – can be productivity tool, **'or'** a major waste of time depending on how you use them. Using your dead time to return calls or keep in touch with the office, your family, or clients can be a great use of your time. Using it to allow clients to get back to you when you need to hear from them or in cases of crisis is great too. Use SMART phones to check and answer email while waiting. There are numerous APS available, with more being added daily. Find which ones will add to your productivity or allow you to use your time more effectively. I love the talking Google Maps one!

I quite frequently use mine when sitting in an airport to call back clients and have actually completed deals on the tarmac. It also allows me to move my 'office' to a nearby coffee shop for a change of scenery and pace. My wife, **Irene** has been teaching me to use Google maps to help me find places I need to visit and to plan my driving route. I have even trained my phone to allow me to use voice commands for hands free calling.

With the advent of additional technology look for these creative 'tools' to become even more interactive with additional Internet connections and applications and even voice activated dictation (getting better) and instantaneous translation into other languages.

CD, DVD, and MP3 players – with so many of us traveling and commuting on a daily basis, using our time wisely here can be a benefit to our ongoing professional development, enjoyment, or inspiration.

A daily commute of 30-45 minutes one way is not unusual for many of us. These same 30-45 minutes can be better used listening to a CD or MP3 of a favorite speaker or educator instead of music. Many of my fellow CAPS and NSA speakers have wonderful recordings; often I pop one in when driving. With a personal digital player or smart phone, these experts can be taken with you on the road or the airways. I travel a fair amount to deliver my programs to clients across North America and around the globe. Sitting in airports used to be a waste of time. I have had some good response from my digital offerings as tools for people in similar situations.

Computers – have become a valuable tool for increased productivity with the ability to store, combine, and deliver information across the world in seconds. I am now able to send contracts, biographical information, and even learning guides as attachments to my clients. This saves time, money, and, most of all, the hassle of printing, compiling, and mailing.

I take a smaller laptop along as I travel to keep in touch with clients, do some writing and surf the net to keep my social media current when I have a few minutes to spare. **Irene** and I have made good use of SKYPE to communicate on the road. This allows me to keep in touch and share what is happening as I travel the globe.

Use of templates has allowed me to systemize my speaking and consulting business so I am able to spend more time on the important activities and with the people I value the most. In fact most of what I need to transact my dealings with clients is on the desktop at home, the laptop I travel with, and on my website, so I can make it easy for clients to say 'YES' to engaging me.

A fellow speaker suggested I spend only 10-12 minutes a day playing with my computer and the various software programs to learn what the various programs can do and what the various helps, short cuts, and macro's, etc do.

We do not need the latest tool or update, but we do need to fully utilize what we have. I am still learning new tips and techniques from my Office components.

> **Taking the time to learn new programs will allow you to better leverage your time investment in technology.**

How about programming your computer to pick news or articles of interest in your particular field of study? This can make your time more productive. Moreover, if you do it with an audio system, it can be downloaded onto an MP3 system and listened to enroute.

Automating – to save keystrokes and using your mouse is a major help if you use the computer a lot. Use of macro's can reduce a name, full sentence, etc to a couple of keystrokes, save time and reduce the chance of misspelling something you frequently type. Use of an auto-correct will help if you commonly miss-type certain words. Learn how to leverage the program assistants and wizards in your creative endeavours.

A Computer backup system – is an essential time management tool. It is not if you will lose data, but 'when', as learned when a worm virus infected my laptop. Backing up on a regular basis is a good investment of your time in managing your data, client information, or, in my instance, my creative efforts. You can program it to do this when you are away or asleep.

Contact management systems – have become more acceptable in our business environment with many companies using them to track data, client information, and schedule contacts and follow-ups. Investigate the various ones and see which one makes sense for your situation. Check out their adaptability. Can they grow with you?

Dictation software – allows you to record digitally and then synchronize with your computer for a transcription. You can also dictate directly to your computer. The downside is they are still slower than normal speech, only 85-90% accurate and require time to train…kind of like a new puppy. Nevertheless, they can be very useful as well. I am working with mine and hope to be able to use it to offer transcripts of my training sessions and talks to my clients and to capture thoughts and creative insights during those sessions.

Digital recorders and cameras – are becoming commonplace and certainly less expensive. Digital recorders are so clear and crisp that it sounds like it was done in a studio. In addition, it can be edited and cleaned up if something happened during the session. Many smart phones have these built in. Digital cameras and smart phones/cameras have gained wider use. They now outsell traditional cameras and have changed the field of photography. They can be an effective communication tool able to capture an image digitally and send it across the world in a matter of seconds. A picture is worth a thousand words, is now digitally even more so!

Internet cloud based storage - is coming into its own. It is gaining acceptance as an effective way to back up or store data and information that can be easily accessed by several people. Look for this to be an effective way of doing catalogues, training manuals, technical manuals, and even e-books.

Drop Box and other online programs – allow you to share information easily with a group of people and to share larger files.

Internet and telephone based meetings – either as audio or video are helping companies increase productivity and allow for interaction over distances. They allow people in various locations to be able to interact, share ideas, and allow for feedback. Our national CAPS board met monthly on call-in bridge lines to discuss issues and make decisions. Our directors lived across Canada and sometimes called in while on the road. This worked well to keep us in touch.

Internet based training – tele-seminars and webinars, and Google hang outs are gaining acceptance for cost and time savings. Like Tele-seminars, it allows people in various locations to be in contact and learn from one another. It saves on travel and accommodations as well as time away from work and home. It will not replace the need to bring people together for training or conferences, but it is a nice, relatively inexpensive, augment to that for follow-up and reinforcement.

Customer service and promotion via Internet – can be a great tool, allowing customers to share concerns and feedback with you and each other. Using Frequently Asked Questions (FAQ) and help tips cuts down on service work and time delays to assist clients in their concerns. I've found mine to be very effective in giving potential clients a snapshot of what I do through the eyes and questions of other clients. Visit: **www.ideaman.net** and check ours out.

PDF files – can be a creative time saver. Create a PDF of commonly disseminated documents. This frees you up to be able to keep your information crisp and current. It can be a nice improvement for on-line catalogues too! We are in the process of converting all our learning guides and printing masters, contracts, and speaker information to PDF format. This will allow us to better service clients while on the road and drastically reduce the time needed to share information or get masters to them for their use in one of our leadership development or other training programs.

These are just a few thoughts on leveraging technology to help you get more done. As said, it is not meant to be a definitive piece of work. We share them with you simply to point out that there are tools and techniques available to help you get control of your life, inject some clarity into your work world and free up time for the people and activities you love.

Meetings, boy do we have meetings

"A committee is a group of men who individually can do nothing, but collectively can meet, and decide that nothing can be done."
Alfred E. Smith

Someone jokingly said, *"Thank God, when He decided the save the world…that He didn't send a committee."* This may seem a bit harsh; but in effectively using our time we may find our commitments to 'meeting-itis' to be a big time waster. Am I saying serving on committees in a waste of time? NO! In fact, the most effective use of our time is by working together to tackle the larger goals we would never accomplish alone.

The National Speakers Association, the Canadian Association of Professional Speakers, or our Global Speakers Federation are concrete examples of professionals banding together to help each other achieve more than they could as individuals. Join a Toastmasters Club and experience firsthand the value of group dynamics and encouragement in your professional growth.

What I am saying, is that having a meeting for the sake of having a meeting or a committee for that purpose, is counterproductive. Know 'WHY' you are meeting and schedule it to be tight and effective. I have come away from countless meetings frustrated and feeling like my time has been wasted or stolen. It doesn't have to be so!

Here are a few of the reasons why we have 'useless' meetings:

- To provide an audience for someone 'important'
- To socialize
- To escape from being effective
- To procrastinate and avoid something we don't want to do
- Habit (we've always had this meeting)
- To pass the buck (easier than making a decision) or to procrastinate
- To fool people into believing they are participating in important decisions

If you become aware that these 'reasons/excuses' exist, find a way to quietly or unobtrusively excuse yourself and go back to work! (Having yourself messaged or called to the phone works! It makes for an easy exit.)

There are good reasons where meetings work better as a method of communication

- Share knowledge
- Establish common goals
- Gain commitment and support from a larger group
- Provide group identity
- Team formation and interaction
- Status forum (part of the in crowd of decision makers)

But how do we keep our meetings effective? Here are some fundamentals learned over the years from countless corporate, community, and association meetings, about the essence of successful meetings.

- **NEED:** Hold 'only' those meeting for which you see a clearly demonstrated need. If you can cover the points by memo, email, fax, or by a call or two, then don't call a meeting. Call a meeting **only** when you have a problem or task that requires the input and on-site assistance of a larger, relevant, or impacted group.

Meetings work best when you need to gather to solve problems that are complex, exchange technical material, or explain policies and procedures that affect a great number of people.

- **PURPOSE**: Each meeting must have a clearly defined object and purpose! Those coming must know in advance what these are. This allows them to be able to prepare and bring any materials that will help the group in reaching or fulfilling this purpose.
- **PARTICIPANTS:** Invite ONLY those people who can really contribute, or have a need to know. The length of a meeting extends in direct proportion to the number of people in attendance 'who have to comment' on the points at hand.

A decade back, I had the opportunity to help establish the first two Home Depot stores in BC. We had weekly managers meetings, which ran conservatively twice the needed length. Our store manager would announce new policies or decisions and then allow everyone around the table to comment on them; and they did! With 35-40 managers, you can imagine why our meetings ran long.

- **AGENDAS:** Pre-circulated Agendas are an absolute, if you wish to be effective with your meetings. Try to circulate the agenda 48 to 72 hours before the meeting, so attendees are prepared and ready to contribute. If all else fails, write the agenda on a white board or flip chart for last minute meetings.

From experience, over 75% of meetings have no preplanned agenda. Any wonder why most of them are ineffective? Agendas 'force' the leader to focus and organize their thoughts and allocate sufficient time for each item. Accountability works!

- **MEETING PLACE:** Work to find a location with good ventilation, comfort, equipment, and proper accessibility. Meet in places free from distractions and interruptions. This is even more important if the purpose of your meeting is to brainstorm or generate creative ideas.

- **PUNCTUALITY - START AND FINISH ON TIME:** This sends a clear signal to participants that their time is valued and they are expected to respect the meeting time. Some suggest starting with a brief uncomplicated activity so late comers can catch up. Don't recap for those who arrive late. They will learn to show up on time, more so, if they have to work at getting the information. Reward the behavior you want - punctuality!

- **STICK TO THE AGENDA:** Encourage participation but make a note and hold over new issues (unless they are really more important than the reason you decided to call the meeting) to another meeting. Don't let the meeting get sidetracked. Keep it on track! As meeting leader, this is your main focus! If you are to make a change, poll the attendees first to see if that is their wish. Agendas are in effect a 'contract' with those who attend. Treat both with respect!

- **LEAD A BALANCED, CONTROLLED DISCUSSION:** As the meeting leader you can 'support members' in expressing their concerns and views, even on volatile or touchy subjects. Steer away from arguments. Don't let one person 'dominate' or manipulate a meeting.

- **SUMMARIZE AND DISTRIBUTE MINUTES**: Recap the decisions and actions planned as a result of the meeting and circulate to those who attended. Make sure they know who is to do what, and by when. Time deadlines and action plans are very effective. Note any follow up or new items for next meeting.

Effective meetings can leverage your time and help, by giving you the forum to share your ideas and gain the support you need to succeed in your life and career. Choose carefully, participate fully, and evaluate your continued involvement, constantly. If you value your time and the time of others, meetings will be 'magic' and motivating.

"Life is about moving, it's about change.
And when things stop doing that they're dead."
Twyla Tharpe

When and where to meet

Here are examples of informal meetings that you might recognize as being more time effective:

- **Impromptu meetings** are great on short notice to discuss issues frankly and to reach decisions quickly without the input of large groups or attendees.
- **Small informal meetings** are useful for discussing, problem-solving, and giving feedback. They are planned so preparation is required, but action can be implemented because of smaller numbers.
- **Brainstorming sessions** are great to generated new ideas or elicit quick ideas for solutions to situational problems.
- **Stand up meetings** or meetings-on-the-run can be a very effective form of decision making, problem solving, and information sharing and gathering. Taking the initiative and seeking out others who need to give input allows you to get in quickly, share relevant information, and make a quick decision.

I remember being invited to visit one of my long-time clients in an Edmonton based large retail operation who had called to discuss a new project for me. I walked into his office and started taking off my winter jacket. He smiled and said, "Don't take it off. You won't be here that long!" We briefly discussed a project he wanted me to undertake, making sure I understood what he wanted and when. He thanked me for coming and I was gone in less than 5 minutes. He valued his time and respected mine as well.

"All who have accomplished great things have had a great aim, have fixed their gaze on a goal, which is high, one, which sometimes seemed impossible."
Orison Swett Marden

Remember:

- Never write a letter, when a memo or email will do.
- Never write a memo, when a phone call will do.
- Never call a meeting when a quick visit or call can accomplish the same results.
- Never call a meeting unless it's the most effective means to accomplish your goals

Value-based decisions

By now you've discovered that gaining control of your time and life will not happen overnight. After all, you didn't lose control overnight. With determination and some diligence in how you allocate your time, you can gradually regain and enhance control of your personal agenda and life.

In my priority based, time management training sessions, I explain that time management is really a series of 'value-based decisions'. The choices we make give 'evidence' to how we value various parts of our lives and the people with whom we share them.

In February, 1999 I spoke at my dad's memorial service. I wanted to speak on behalf of the family and most specifically as his son, about how much he had meant to us. I shared how he had modeled love, compassion, and commitment to service.

"Time is too precious to waste and the people we invest it in are too precious for us not to invest it with them!"

Dad wasn't a hero in the comic book sense of the word, but he was 'my hero'! He showed me how it was done. That was part of his legacy and the time he invested in me. I remember telling those assembled that if you wanted to see what he valued, then take a walk through his checkbook and his appointment calendar.

In another perspective, take a look at how a person 'actually' values and uses their time by taking a walk through their schedule. Our actions, however misguided or well-intentioned, reveal what we 'truly' value. If you tell me you are committed to and value building a retirement fund; then show me a systematic track record of savings and growth, however small. If you tell me you're committed to and value personal or professional growth; show me the courses, books, and MP3s where you've invested your time and resources.

If you tell me you are committed to and value relationships; show me time spent with the people you value. After Dad died, my mom, who was already sick, needed a lot more care. It was my privilege to be flexible in my role as a speaker to be able to take regular, extended, time off to tend to her needs. I had the privilege, along with my sister, of being able to hold her in my arms as she passed away. As mentioned earlier, I'd do it again in a heartbeat!

Many years ago, I had a brief stint as a financial planner. I found it challenging and valuable in the insights and information I was able to bring to my client's lives, families, and finances.

One of the basic tenets of good financial management is 'spend less than you earn!' One more important one was the importance of 'paying yourself first' as a form of self-management investment in your financial future.

I was amazed at how few people applied this simple little technique, a principle that has proven invaluable in providing solid investments and retirement income. Again, a sense of bad value-based decisions in paying other people first; and trying to live, save, and invest on the left-overs. The result is that most people cannot afford to retire! Invest in yourself first and make sure you set aside time for you!

The principle works in time allotment too! Always, schedule time for yourself first! This will ensure the activities and people you truly value will have the time you want them to have. Make this value your passion! A simple idea, but a very powerful one. Why not value yourself as highly as you would those around you.

Like, *'Love your neighbor as yourself!'* But, you have to love yourself first to be able to truly love your neighbor or your family or your career.

We challenge you to take a few minutes to think about what you really value in the various areas of your life. This is different than the priority exercise, in that priorities change, but values tend to be a little more anchored. This can be a very crucial investment of your time if you are truly serious in regaining control of your time and life and in being more productive.

What do you value in each of these categories? I trust you will enjoy this process!

- **Personal**

- **Time**

- **Family**

- Spouse/Partner

- Kids/grandkids

- Career

- Community

- Professional development

- Pleasure

- Financial

- Spiritual

- Material/possessions

- Personal legacy

- Other

When you are aware and sensitive of what you really value, it makes it easier to schedule your high-value *priorities* and say 'NO' to the time wasters and people in your life.

These are not designed to be the definitive list; simply a memory jog for you as you take a moment to decide what you really value in life in each of these areas. You might also take a moment to rank or re-organize them in relation to their importance and value in your life. The challenge after you've done this exercise is to go back through your priorities with these 'values' in hand. See if, in fact, your values are reflected in your actions. The value here is to then schedule based on what you actually value.

We wish you a speedy 'recovery' in your quest to regain your time and your life. It will be a challenge, but it can be done!

Secrets of a procrastinator - It's about time!

"Next time, I'm not going to leave it until the last minute." Ever said that?

I have and all too often - in the past! Ever notice how that happens? We start off with all sorts of good intentions and somehow we end up rushing, under pressure, stressed to complete a task that would have been a breeze, if ONLY, we had done it earlier.

"At times," said **Emerson**, *"the whole world seems to be in a conspiracy to importune you - with emphatic trifles."*

The secret, in the midst of our often hectic, fast paced, activity driven life is in our discerning and sidestepping those trivial demands; to remain focused and active on the important ones vs. the urgent ones.

"TODAY, is an important day!" according to **Zig Ziglar**, *"No matter how you spend it, you will have traded a day of your life for it!"* Based on an improved age span of 85 years, we have ONLY 31,046 days to LIVE! Roughly 745,000 hours in which to live out our dreams, accomplish our life goals, and make an impact on our world and those with whom we share it.

"Do you love life? Then do not squander time," said **Benjamin Franklin**; *"for TIME is the stuff that life is made of."*

As a recovering PROCRASTINATOR, I offer these **four suggestions** to help control and conquer time, and truly live your life.

DEVOTE time to your goals. Make sure you know where it is you really want to go, what you really want to accomplish, and what impact statement you want your life to make. Spend time analyzing, refining, and prioritizing. As little as 15 minutes a day could impact a lifetime. Make sure these goals are realistic and compatible with your life message. Then get on with them. DO IT NOW!

LEARN TO LEVERAGE your time by networking with others, by delegating or sharing tasks, by asking colleagues for help, and by seeking their energy, information, and resource sharing.

CREATE TIME like **Thomas Edison** who set aside a 'portion' of each day for the creative processes. Use this designated creative time to brainstorm, mind map goals and objectives, and to reflect on the organization, timing, and implementation of your goals. Use this creative time to dream BIG and leverage visualization techniques to allow yourself to establish your own pace and direction.

DON'T WASTE YOUR TIME. How many of us, could find at least 15-20 minutes a day that we now squander? According to Goethe, *"One always has enough time, provided one spends it well" What difference would that make?*

Your life and time management is in your hands. It is within your power to choose to invest it well for your benefit and the benefit of those you love. Or, you can choose to let others rob you of your life's blood or squander it on useless pursuits. It is your choice - and it's about time!

But what if you find yourself overwhelmed with commitments? How do I get out from under them you may ask? We'll give you an idea on the next page, so keep reading my friend.

Tap into the power of your bedroom

My friend and co-author, **Guy Kawasaki** warns of the danger of skipping sleep and its resulting *negative* impact on your productivity. As he shared, "We all skip sleep from time to time to make a tight deadline or fix an emergency. It's unavoidable, but resist the temptation to burn the midnight oil for tasks that aren't urgent. Getting six hours of sleep instead of seven robs you of **'two-and-a-third to three hours'** worth of productivity in an eight-hour workday - longer if you're pulling the 12-hour shifts of many business owners."

Getting enough sleep is *critical* to having the mental and physical energy needed to productively work through your day. Start getting ready for bed at least an hour before you actually do. Disengage from 'all' your electronics; TV, phone, internet. Read a book, listen to music, soak, or have a glass of wine with your spouse and allow yourself to relax.

Ever wake up during the night with an idea or concern running in your brain and can't get back to sleep? I get up and brain dump on a piece of paper, in my journal, or on my computer. Then as my minds clears I go back to bed and continue my sleep, un-encumbered and relaxed.

The Power of UN-Commitment!

Ever find yourself overcommitted, 'facing the reality' of not being able to do what you've promised in the time you have available? Ever find yourself moving a task repeatedly each day to your already overcrowded TO DO list? What would you do? How do you handle this seemingly impossible situation?

The harsh reality is someone (often yourself) is going to be disappointed. However, there is a solution!

- Simply take a few moments to list and review your commitments.
- Then, decide which ones you want to finish or can and will finish within your agreed deadline.
- If something has been repeatedly postponed ask yourself if you really want to do it? Be honest now! If you don't, then stop re-scheduling it.
- Take a moment and revisit your priorities. Make sure you evaluate your continued commitments based on what you've decided you want to accomplish in the various parts of your life.

This is time to make some changes.

Final step: After you've determined a realistic commitment to what you can and will finish; screw up your courage and call those people who are involved and inform them that you are unable to complete the task you promised them. They will find out anyway when it doesn't get done on time.

Remember, if you tell them in advance it's a reason; if you tell them after the deadline, it's an excuse. Excuses don't cut it in business or relationships. Why make two people worry and one mad?

Getting free and regaining control of your life requires making some tough choices. If you don't make them decisively and follow through, you will never reach the level of freedom you desire. In the long run, your ability to allocate your time for the important people and activities in your life is paramount.

 "Time is the coin of your life. It is the only coin you have, and only you can determine how it will be spent. Be careful lest you let other people spend it for you." Carl Sandburg

Time Wasters – The Dirty Dozen
Developed originally for executives & administrative assistants

For this specialized time management section people in support positions were polled and asked for their 'dirty dozen' time wasters. We asked them to share in confidence and were amazed by what they told us.

This section was originally focused for executive and administrative assistants in a program conducted for a local college in Vancouver, BC. We realized it was helpful for their leaders and executives too. Perhaps you might catch a glimpse of where you, as a leader, may not as helpful in working with your assistants and teams as you would like to be.

They are:

1. Lack of adequate planning
2. My boss's procrastination and lack of attention to making or following through on decisions
3. Incompetent subordinates and co-workers (might be a training issue?)
4. My inability to say NO or set boundaries (need to be honest about workloads and setting priorities)
5. Interruptions – drop-in visitors
6. Interruptions – telephone
7. Indecision
8. My procrastination
9. Forgetfulness
10. Meetings (not needed or poorly organized)
11. My challenge with perfectionism
12. Failure to delegate

Take a minute and think about these dirty dozen. I challenge you to commit to being conscious of them as you work with your assistants and colleagues. Dedicated to my amazing supportive friends **Bridgette Dunphy, Corina MacFayden**, and **Sandra Miko** who help keep their respective leaders productively on track and on target. Ask your assistant to help you as you work on them.

In fact, why not go the extra mile and buy them their own copy of **'*Running TOO Fast?'*** Then both of you can discuss it from time to time as you work on it together.

How to avoid 'upward' delegation

One of the bigger challenges leaders face is having problems and challenges dumped in their laps. What makes it worse – some leaders actively take on challenges which need to be delegated to someone more qualified. Sadly they allow their staff to delegate upward and add to their already bulging workload. This is the reverse of effective leadership.

Effective delegation is an essential leadership skill; one that is forged and learned in the heat of over-commitment and the struggle to be productive. To avoid the 'upward' delegation from subordinates and co-workers; be ready to ask them to answer the following questions 'before' you and/or your immediate boss get involved.

1. Give me a clear statement of the problem, challenge, or idea.
2. What alternatives have you uncovered or researched?
3. What are the advantages and disadvantages for each of them?
4. What is your best recommendation to solve this challenge or to implement this idea and 'Why?' or 'What is the next step and why?'

It will take a while if you have been the 'delegation-dumping' place for your office, but it will change when you set some *realistic* boundaries and challenge them to be responsible. You'll find that they will soon get the message:

"Don't bring me a problem or challenge until you've done your homework and can help make a reasoned recommendation or decision."

Another time waster is 'useless' questions. Don't be afraid to make them do some homework first.

While serving as District 21 Governor for BC's Toastmasters (1997-1998), I called the World Headquarters and asked a question. Stan Stills took my call and was very gracious the 'first' time. I remember him saying, *"Bob, do you have your District Leadership Manual?"* He continued, *"Let's see if we can find the answer to your question together."* We did! He was very gracious; but, I soon discovered he needed me to do my homework first. Often, the answer was in the book and I only had to call when it wasn't specifically referenced or recorded.

I'd suggest doing something like that with those who report to you or those co-workers who come to you as the office 'resource' person.

4 questions that can help save you time

Q1: Could the 'answer' be found in meeting notes, files, or policies and procedures manuals?
Q2: Could another staff member or co-worker answer it?
Q3: Does it simply need a 'yes' or 'no' answer? Can that be handled by a quick phone call?
Q4: Is it a (type) question that 'really' requires your personal attention? (This could be a training issue for future reference.)

Here are some tips on dealing with two top time wasters

Dealing with Drop-In Visitors

This can be the toughest challenge in any office environment, more so with the advent of the open office layout and 'open door' policy. But you can get a handle on it, if you are willing to do a little changing in your response to people and in how you interact as a leader or top performing professional.

Perhaps you could revisit the 'open door' policy and designate periods during the day when your door is closed and people are taught that this is 'don't interrupt me unless it is a REAL emergency' time. Learn to develop defined signals and try to move them out of your office or work area. For example, stand up and walk with them in the direction of another area.

Take a strategic look at your office or work area. Are you sitting so you make easy eye contact with people as they pass by? Is there a natural conversation area or a place for them to sit or perch? Do you have a clock where it is easily seen? Perhaps you need to rearrange your office and workspace to help keep the distractions to a minimum?

Encourage your subordinates and co-workers to use 'save-up' files and not interrupt as often. Don't be afraid to tell them you don't have a minute to spare and ask if you can reschedule for later in the day or another time. You may find the problem got solved in the meantime.

Work to consolidate visitors and mini-meetings to save time disruptions. It is always easier to do several related things at a time than to jump back and forth between activities. Establish a 'quiet time' and make sure your co-workers and subordinates know about it. This can be transforming.

If applicable, get your immediate boss to buy-in as well. If you pitch it to your boss as a time in which you focus and deal with the creative issues on his/her behalf you may find it an easier sell.

Leaders: Suggest that your assistants do a little horse-trading with a fellow assistant or co-worker to cover their/your calls and to run interference for you. Even 15 minutes of quiet, uninterrupted, focused time can be tremendously effective and productive.

Handling the phone-in time wasters

Here are a few tips that might help your assistant get a handle on the phone-in time wasters in your day. If you answer your own phone, you might get someone to cover for you on occasion or see where you can apply these tips we share with administrative or executive assistants.

Here is what we suggest as ways to be more productive:

- Screen your boss's calls and set up a hit list (always gets through, never gets through, or allow through at your discretion).
- Have your boss return their own calls where possible. Give him/her an outline of the question or message so they are well prepared!
- Don't ask open ended questions. Be specific and get the information needed for a quick call back by you or your boss.
- Use a call back system and consolidate your calls. Develop a script or agenda first! (This is a true time saver!)
- Avoid telephone tag: Make a specific phone appointment and/or leave a detailed voice mail. This one is my favorite. I phone someone and leave a 'specific' voice mail asking for 'specific' information. They phone back and leave a message, *"I'm returning your call!"* Drives me crazy.

Dirty Dozen is excerpted is from Bob's *"Success Skills for leaders, entrepreneurs, and those who support them."* We'll be updating it later this year in an e-pub format. When you apply these tips you will be more productive and so will those who support you.

'Carpe Momento' – Seize the Moment!

How many of us are so busy planning, scheming, dreaming about the future, or rehashing the past that we miss the moment? If you are like me, you've probably been there from time to time.

Remember waking up one day and wondering what you actually did or accomplished the day before? Or at the end of the day, asking yourself the same question? You were busy, that you remember; but you can't remember what you were busy doing. Sound familiar?

> *"Our main business is not to see what lies dimly at a distance, but to do what lies clearly at hand."*
> **Thomas Carlyle**

Some have heard the phrase, **'Carpe Diem' – Seize the Day!** I would venture that we need to go even further than that and **Seize the Moment! – 'Carpe Momento'.** (*Ok so I made the phrase up – but, it makes sense, doesn't it?*)

It is what we do during the moments of each day that contribute to the end result of the day. Was it a good one, which energized you? Was it one, which left you unsettled, unsatisfied, and unproductive? The choice is yours, on a moment-by-moment basis.

In 1913, **Sir William Osler** was asked to address the students at Yale University. Sir William had earned acclaim by organizing the John Hopkins School of Medicine and being appointed Regius Professor of Medicine at Oxford and been Knighted by the King of England. It would appear he had earned the right to share a few ideas with that student body.

He attributed his success to reading something from Thomas Carlyle 40 some years earlier, which had helped him keep focused, and to live in 'day-tight' compartments. He shared how he had crossed the Atlantic on an ocean liner and had seen how it was compartmentalized in case of emergency. He noticed each compartment could be shut off quickly.

He challenged them to live their lives in what he called 'day-tight' compartments. He challenged them to *"Shut off the past."* He went on to say, *"Shut off the future as tightly as the past… the future is today."*

I learned firsthand about the concept of 'day-tight' compartments in the 1980's, when I went through a divorce. A divorce that left me 'disillusioned' with my life; feeling a bit of a failure and that my life had little real meaning or purpose. I had married later in life, intending to make it a 'forever' commitment – unfortunately forever was only 7 years. I was struggling for a sense of purpose, of hope, and understanding how this could have gotten so sidetracked. Each day was a chore and a challenge.

I left the 'family' business when the marriage ended and was at a loss for what to do at that moment. I saw an ad for a little run down coffee shop in New Westminster, BC. I drove over, took a peek, and negotiated to buy it. It had been closed for 5 months and needed extensive work before it could reopen. I spent over 6 weeks working on cleaning it up, scrapping, deep cleaning, re-wiring, revamping and remodeling; making sure I had the tools and menu designed so we could reopen. Each day was a struggle, both in focus and finances, in creating my idea to provide something that would prove of value.

It was heartbreaking work, back breaking too. When the **'Cubbyhole' Café** opened that fall, it became a place where people who worked in the area and tourists could stop for a break, some good food, and good conversation. It was not easy as we struggled to build a clientele and to gain exposure in that area of town. I worked to maintain a positive attitude, to be a gracious host, and warmly welcome my guests each day. There were days I was so tired, that I would pray, *"Lord, just help me make it through to lunch"* or *"Lord, help me make it to closing time."*

The days blended into each other, and one day I noticed that I had gotten through the day without challenge. I was re-gaining my confidence and clarity. As I fed my mind with *positive* ideas and reached out to people, I found myself growing again. I had found that each day was taking care of itself, providing challenge and enjoyment, as I took care to be in the moment and live it fully.

I sold the 'Cubbyhole' a couple of years later; began a consulting business and a return to my kitchen design practice prior to moving into speaking and training. The lessons I learned at the 'Cubbyhole' will live with me forever. When I focused on being 'in the moment', in seizing each opportunity, and wringing out all the life it had, the days took care of themselves.

Note: I joined Toastmasters International during this time and found the time invested in attending meetings, learning to speak, and honing my leadership skills to be very helpful. More so as I rebuilt my confidence and expertise and gained valuable experience as a leader.

On Feb 11th, 1999 my dad passed away peacefully in his sleep. One moment he was alive and the next he was with the Lord. That moment impacted me deeper than I could have ever expected. My dad had been my anchor and my greatest cheerleader. I struggled to deal with this loss and to assist my mom in continuing her life and dealing with his devastating loss of her husband.

A bit over six months later, on **August 20th, 1999,** I held my mom in my arms (my sister held her hand) and watched as she too slipped away. One moment alive and struggling valiantly to breathe - the next moment, at peace, and on her way to be with Dad. I cherish each moment of time I spent with Mom and Dad. I treasure the moments taken to care for her, after Dad left us. I would not trade a moment, not even the smallest one, for all the income in the world.

2001, September 11th, our world was changed in a moment when terrorists crashed two large jets into the World Trade Center in New York and another into the Pentagon. Our sense of values was changed, our sense of safety was impacted, and the way we do business was changed – in a moment! We were hard hit in the speaking and training industry as thousands of regional meetings and national conferences were instantly cancelled. I had three cancel and one put on hold in the next two weeks.

It remained to be seen how the impact would wash out, but many of us worked at maintaining a sense of balance and focus, moment by moment. We faced an uncertain future for our industry. We were confident that our skills, our words, and our experience would continue to instill value in the lives of our potential clients, readers, and audiences. Our voices were still needed! Life needed to go on, business needed to continue, and people's needs still needed to be cared for!

I was speaking in New Jersey, across the Hudson River from NYC, that December 2001. I took a morning to travel over and walk around 'Ground Zero'. It was a walk of quiet reflection, of being in the moment, and allowing the sense of tragedy and loss to impact me.

I took time to stop and read the cards, the 'have you seen this man, or my daughter, or wife, or sister?' notes. I found myself in tears several times along the path. A chance to take a moment and read the patriotic notes; the declarations of optimism and hope that people from around the world had left on the walls and fences surrounding the area. To take a moment of reflection and leave my thoughts on the wall, and a dedication that *"I too would continue to speak out, to encourage people to live their lives, enhance their careers, contribute to their communities, and to give and to gain the riches each moment would bring."* "To bring HOPE and HELP to my audiences!"

Dante wrote, *"Think, this day will never dawn again."* Each moment, when passed is gone forever, lost in the sands of time. Each moment is like a grain of sand which when it has passed through the narrow neck of the hourglass of our life, cannot be returned or reused. There is no do-over!

It is the decisions and the dedication in which we 'invest' our moments in time, which determine the richness of our life and legacy. These decisions impact our life, our careers, and those we love.

- Decide 'today' to live in the moment, make each moment count in your life and the lives of those you value.
- Decide 'today' to let yesterday take care of itself, to plan for the future, but live for today.
- Decide 'today' to value yourself and your time highly, and to invest yourself in a worthy cause.

The time you spend will continue to prove valuable, to you and to those you lead. Talking time to encourage them, train them, and inspire them is time well spent! I've shared some of my past struggles with you for a number of reasons.

- I know there are people who are hurting, confused, and conflicted about the pressures and challenges of life. I share my struggles and successes as a bridge to build bonds and to offer encouragement that they, too, can move through and win.
- Being in management has its rewards. However, it can be a very demanding and challenging time too. It can also be very lonely and frustrating at times.
- Being a leader is a worthy vocation. Taking personal leadership in how you allocate your time so you can be active. Helping people improve their businesses and their lives is the positive result of professionals like you.

Bob's B.E.S.T. publications

Bob is a *prolific* author who has been capturing and sharing his wisdom and experience in printed and electronic formats for the past fifteen plus years. In addition to the following publications, several of them best sellers; he has written for consumer, corporate, professional associations, trade, and on-line publications. He has been engaged to write and assist on publications by other best-selling writers and successful companies. His publications are listed to give you an idea of the scope and topics he writes about. Bob's **B**usiness **E**nhancement **S**uccess **T**ools.

Leadership, business, and career development series

- **Running TOO Fast?** (7th edition updated 2014)
- **Legacy of Leadership** (2nd Edition 2013)
- **Make ME Feel Special!** Secrets of Exceptional Customer Service (2014)
- Why Didn't I 'THINK' of That? (updated 2014)
- **Speaking for Success!** (7th Edition updated 2012)
- A Quest for Balance (SFS companion)
- **Creating TIME to Sell, Lead, or Manage** (2nd Edition 2012)
- Thinking Beyond the FIRST Sale
- Create the Future!
- CONFLICT - Dealing effectively with conflict
- Get to YES! - The subtle art of persuasion in negotiation (EPUB)
- For Immediate Release – The Personal Power of Public Relations
- Media Management - What to say if a reporter calls
- Winning in the Boardroom – Maximized meetings that get results
- THINK Before You Ink! (EPUB)
- Running to Win! (EPUB)
- Coaching for Optimal Results
- Success Skills for leaders, entrepreneurs, and those who support them

Bob's Mini-book series

- TALK, So People Will Listen

- The Courage to Lead!
- LEAD, So People Will Follow
- Creativity Counts!
- How to Generate More Sales
- Success - Sampler and Companion
- Unleash your Business Potential
- My 'Next' Million Dollar Idea Book
- Learn to Listen
- Thanks Mom!
- Dad, You're Still My Hero!

Bob's Pocket Wisdom series

- Pocket Wisdom for Selling Professionals
- Pocket Wisdom for Speakers
- Pocket Wisdom for Innovators
- Pocket Wisdom for Leaders – Power of One!
- Pocket Wisdom for Business Builders
- Additional PW books are coming in 2014

Co-authored e-books created by Bob
- Quantum Success – 3 volume series
- **In The Company of Leaders** (2nd Edition 2014)
- **Foundational Success** (2nd Edition 2013)
- A new one to be released in 2014

Visit: www.SuccessPublications.ca for more information on Bob's publications and other success resources.

Want to empower your team? Ask about our volume discount packages for 'Running TOO Fast?' Write us at: bob@ideaman.net

"If you don't write when you don't have time for it, you won't write when you do have time for it."
Katerina Stoykova Klemer

If I had waited for inspiration to strike, few of these publications would have seen the light of day. Over the years I have taught myself to sit and write and then go back and edit and re-write. Eventually something gets 'close enough' and it goes to print. Then, somewhere down the road it gets updated, as I did with *'Running TOO Fast?'* and re-written again.

Thanks for purchasing and reading
'Running TOO Fast? Creating time to lead and still have a life'!

Each time I prepare to step on the stage; each time I sit down to write or in this case to re-write, I am challenged to deliver something that will be of use-it-now value to my audience/reader.

- I ask myself, *"If I was reading this, what value would I be looking for?"*
- As well as, *"Why is this relevant to me, today?"*

These two questions help to keep me focused and clear on my objectives. They help to remind me to dig into my experiences, stories, examples, and research to provide solid information that will be of benefit and help our readers, when they apply it, succeed. That can be an exciting challenge!

I trust we have done that for you in this updated primer on more effective communication and presentation skills. *'Running TOO Fast?'* is my attempt to capture some of the lessons learned first-hand from observing and working with some tremendously effective leaders and to share them with you.

I'd love to hear from you and read your success stories. If you would be so kind, please drop me a quick email at: **bob@ideaman.net**

Bob 'Idea Man' Hooey
2011 Spirit of CAPS recipient
www.ideaman.net
www.HaveMouthWillTravel.com

Connect with me on:

- **Facebook:** www.facebook.com/bob.hooey
- **LinkedIn:** www.linkedin.com/in/canadianideamanbobhooey
- **YouTube:** www.youtube.com/ideamanbob
- **Smashwords:** www.smashwords.com/profile/view/Hooey
- **Follow me on Twitter:** @IdeamanHooey
- **Snail mail:** Box 10, Egremont, Alberta T0A0Z0

About the author

Bob 'Idea Man' Hooey is a charismatic, confident leader, corporate trainer, inspiring facilitator, Emcee, prolific author, and award winning motivational keynote speaker on leadership, creativity, success, business innovation, and enhancing team performance.

Using personal stories drawn from rich experience, he challenges his audiences to engage his **Ideas At Work!** – To act on what they hear, with clear, innovative building-blocks and field-proven success techniques to increase their effectiveness. Bob challenges them to hone specific 'success skills' critical to their personal and professional advancement.

Bob outlines real-life, results-based, innovative ideas personally drawn from 29 plus years of rich leadership experience in retail, construction, small business, entrepreneurship, manufacturing, association, consulting, community service, and commercial management.

Bob's conversational, often humorous, professional, and sometimes-provocative style continues to inspire and challenge his audiences across North America. Bob's motivational, innovative, challenging, and practical **Ideas At Work!** have been successfully applied by thousands of leaders and professionals across the globe. Busy man – productive man!

Bob is a frequent contributor to North American consumer, corporate, association, trade, and on-line publications on leadership, success, employee motivation and training; as well as creativity and innovative problem solving, priority and time management, and effective customer service. He is the inspirational author of 30 plus publications, including several best-selling, print, e-books, reader style e-pubs, and a Pocket Wisdom series.

Visit: **www.SuccessPublications.ca** for more information.

123

Retired, award winning kitchen designer, Bob Hooey, CKD-Emeritus was one of only 75 Canadian designers to earn this prestigious certification by the National Kitchen and Bath Association.

In December 2000, Bob was given a special CAPS National Presidential award **"…for his energetic contribution to the advancement of CAPS and his living example of the power of one"** in addition to being elected to the CAPS National Board. He has been recognized by the National Speakers Association and other groups for his leadership contributions.

Bob is a co-founder and a Past President of the CAPS Vancouver Chapter and served as 2012 President of the CAPS Edmonton Chapter. He is a member of the NSA-Arizona Chapter and an active leader in the National Speakers Association, a charter member of the Canadian Association of Professional Speakers, as well as the Global Speakers Federation. He has just retired (December 2013) as a Trustee from the CAPS Foundation.

In 1998, Toastmasters International recognized Bob **"…for his professionalism and outstanding achievements in public speaking"**. That August in Palm Desert, California Bob became the 48th speaker in the world to be awarded this prestigious professional level honor as an **Accredited Speaker**. He has been inducted into their Hall of Fame on numerous occasions for his leadership contributions.

Bob has been honoured by the United Nations Association of BC (1993) and received the **CANADA 125 award** (1992) for his ongoing leadership contributions to the community. In 1998, Bob joined 3 other men to sail a 65 foot gaff rigged schooner from Honolulu, Hawaii to Kobe, Japan, barely surviving a 'baby' typhoon enroute.

In November 2011 Bob was awarded the Spirit of CAPS at their annual convention, becoming the 11th speaker to earn this prestigious CAPS National award. Visit: **www.ideaman.net/SoC.htm**

Bob loves to travel and his speaking and writing have allowed him to visit 41 countries so far. Perhaps your organization would like to bring Bob in to share a few ideas with your leaders and teams around the globe.

Visit: **www.HaveMouthWillTravel.com** for more information.

Acknowledgements, credits, and disclaimers

As with each of my books, a very special dedication of this piece of myself, to the two people who meant the most to me, my folks **Ron and Marge Hooey**. Sadly, both my parents left this earthly realm in 1999. I still miss our time together and your encouragement and love. I was blessed with the two of you in my life.

תודה
Dankie Gracias
Спасибо شکراً
Merci Takk
Köszönjük Terima kasih
Grazie Dziękujemy Děkojame
Ďakujeme Vielen Dank Paldies
Kiitos Täname teid 谢谢
Thank You Tak
感谢您 Obrigado Teşekkür Ederiz
Σας Ευχαριστούμε 감사합니다
ขอบคุณ
Bedankt Děkujeme vám
ありがとうございます
Tack

To my inspiring wife and professional proof reader and publications coach, **Irene Gaudet**, who loves, encourages, and supports me in my quest to continue sharing my **Ideas At Work!** across the world. Thank you seems so inadequate for your timely work in helping make my writing and my client service better! I love the time we spend together!

My thanks to the many people who have encouraged me in my growth as a leader, speaker, and engaging trainer in each area of expertise including *'Running TOO Fast?'*

- To my colleagues and friends in the National Speakers Association **(NSA)**, the Canadian Association of Professional Speakers **(CAPS)**, and the Global Speakers Federation **(GSF)** who continually challenge me to strive for success and increased excellence.
- To my friend **Harold Taylor** for his timely tips, insights, and support.
- To my many **Toastmasters** friends and family around the world, to whom I owe an un-payable debt of gratitude for your investment, encouragement, time, and support when I was just starting down this path; and oh, so rough around the edges.
- **To my great audiences, leaders, students, coaching clients, and readers across the globe** who share their experiences and enjoyment of my work. Your positive and supportive feedback encourages me to keep working on additional programs and success publications like this updated version. My experience with you creates the foundation for additional real-life experiences I can take from the stage to the page, the classroom to the boardroom.
- My thanks to a *select* few friends for your ongoing support and 'constructive' abuse. You know who you are. ☺

Disclaimer

We have not attempted to cite all the authorities and sources consulted in the preparation of this book. To do so would require much more space than is available. The list would include departments of various governments, libraries, industrial institutions, periodicals, and many individuals. Inspiration was drawn from many sources, including other books by the author; in this updated creation of *'Running TOO Fast?'*

This book is written and designed to provide information on more effective use of your time, as a life and leadership enhancement guide. It is sold with the 'explicit' understanding that the publisher and/or the author are **not** engaged in rendering legal, accounting, or other professional services. If legal or other expert assistance is required, the services of a competent professional in your geographic area should be sought.

It is not the purpose of this book to reprint all the information that is otherwise available. Its primary purpose is to complement, amplify, and supplement other books and reference materials already available. You are encouraged to search out and study all the available material, learn as much as possible, and tailor the information to your individual needs. This will help to enhance your success in being a more effective leader or professional.

Every effort has been made to make this book as complete and as accurate as possible within the scope of its focus. However, there may be mistakes, both typographical and in content or attribution. Graphics are royalty free or under license. Care has been taken to trace ownership of copyright material contained in this volume. The publisher will gladly receive information that will allow him to rectify any reference or credit line in subsequent editions. This book should be used only as a general guide and not as the ultimate source of information. Furthermore, this book contains information that is current only up to the date of publication.

The purpose of *'Running TOO Fast?'* is to educate and entertain; perhaps to inform and to inspire. It is certainly to challenge its readers to learn and apply its secrets and tips, to challenge them to enhance their skills and leverage their time to create more productive outcomes.

The author and publisher shall have **neither** liability **nor** responsibility to any person or entity with respect to any loss or damage caused, or alleged to have been caused, directly or indirectly, by the information contained in this book.

What they say about Bob 'Idea Man' Hooey

As I travel across North America, and more recently around the globe, sharing my **Ideas At Work!** I am fortunate to get feedback and comments from my audiences and colleagues. These comments come from people who have been touched, challenged, or simply enjoyed themselves in one of my sessions.

I'd love to come and share some ideas with your organization and teams.

"I've known Bob for several years and follow his activities in business with interest. I originally met Bob when he spoke for a Rotary Leadership Institute and got to know him better when he came to Vladivostok, Russia to speak to our leadership. **When you spoke I thought you were one of us because you talked about our challenges just like yours.** *You could understand the others, which makes you a great speaker!"* **Andrey Konyushok**, *Rotary International District 2225 Governor 2012-2013, far eastern Russia*

"I still get comments from people about your presentation. **Only a few speakers have left an impression that lasts that long.** *You hit a spot with the tourism people."* **Janet Bell**, *Yukon Economic Forums*

"We greatly appreciate **the energy and effort you put into researching and adapting your keynote to make it more meaningful to our member councils.** *Early feedback from our delegates indicates that this year's convention was one of our most successful events yet, and we thank you for your contribution to this success."* **Larry Goodhope**, *Executive Director Alberta Association of Municipal Districts and Counties*

"Thank you Bob; it is **always a pleasure to see a true professional at work.** *You have made the name 'Speaker' stand out as a truism - someone who encourages people to examine their lives and make adjustments. The personal stories you shared with your audience made such a great impression on everyone.* **The comments indicated you hit people right where it is important - in their hearts.** *Each of those in your audience took away a new feeling of personal success and encouragement."* **Sherry Knight**, *Dimension Eleven Human Resources and Communications*

"Bob is one of those rare individuals who knows how to tackle obstacles in life to reach his dreams. He takes each as a learning experience and stretches for more. **His compassion and genuine interest in others make him an exceptional coach."** Cindy Kindret, *Training Manager, Silk FM Radio*

*"Without doubt, **I have gained immeasurable self-assurance.** Bob, your patience and your encouragement has been much appreciated. **I strongly recommend your course to anyone looking for self-improvement and professional development.**"* **Jeannie Mura**, *Human Resources Chevron Canada*

*"I am pleased to recommend Bob 'Idea Man' Hooey to any organization looking for a charismatic, confident speaker and seminar leader. I have seen Bob in action on several occasions, and he is ALWAYS on! Bob has the ability to grab his audience's attention and keep it. Quite simply, **if Bob is involved - your program or seminar is guaranteed to succeed.**"* **Maurice Laving**, *Coordinator Training and Development, London Drugs*

*"I have found **Bob's attention to detail** and his ability to fine tune his seminars to match the time frame and needs of the audience to be a valuable asset to our educational program."* **Patsy Schell**, *Executive Director Surrey Chamber of Commerce*

*"Great seeing you in Cancun and congratulations on a job well done.**The seminar was a great success! Your humorous and conversational style was a tremendous asset.** It is my sincere hope that we can be associated again at future seminars."* **Donald MacPherson**, *Attorney At Law, Phoenix, Arizona*

*"**What a great conference.** It was a great pleasure meeting with you at the Ritz Carlton, Cancun and I shall look forward to hopefully welcoming you and your family in Dublin, Ireland someday."* **A. Paul Ryan**, *Petronva Corporation, Dublin, Ireland*

*"Congratulations on the **Spirit of CAPS Award.** You have worked long and hard on behalf of CAPS ...**helped many speakers including me** and richly deserve this award. Well done my friend."* **Peter Legge**, *CSP, Hof, CPAE*

*"I had the pleasure of hearing and watching Bob Hooey deliver a keynote speech several years ago when he gave a presentation at a Toastmasters International Convention. **Bob impressed me greatly with his professionalism, energy, and ability to connect with his audience while giving them value.** I heartily recommend this talented speaker and 'Idea Man' to all who want to move to the next level."* **Dr. Dilip Abayasekara, DTM, Accredited Speaker,** *Past Toastmasters International President*

*"I attended **Speaking for Success** in Edmonton. **The mark of a true leader is someone who will lay down their own pride to teach all they know to their potential successors.** To be taught by a man of his caliber was an honor whether you're a beginner like myself or a professional; the experience is well worth it! To Bob - it truly was an honor to meet you. Stay humble and enjoy the great success."*
Samantha McLeod

Engage Bob for your leaders and their teams

"I have been so excited working with Bob Hooey, as he has given inspiration and motivation to our leadership team members. Both at the Brick Warehouse – Alberta and here at Art Van Furniture – Michigan; with his years of experience in working with business executives and his humorous and delightful packaging of his material, he makes learning with Bob a real joy. But most importantly, anyone who comes in contact with his material is the better for it."
Kim Yost, CEO Art Van Furniture, former CEO The Brick

Motivate your teams, your employees, and your leaders to 'productively' grow and 'profitably' succeed!

- Protect your conference investment - leverage your training dollars.
- Enhance your professional career and sell more products and services.
- Equip and motivate your leaders and their teams to grow and succeed, 'even' in tough times!
- Leverage your time to enhance your skills, equip your teams, and better serve your clients.
- Leverage your leadership and investment of time to leave a significant legacy!

Call today to engage best-selling author, award winning, inspirational leadership keynote speaker, leaders success coach, and employee development trainer, **Bob 'Idea Man' Hooey** and his innovative, audience based, results-focused, **Ideas At Work!** for your next company, convention, leadership, staff, training, or association event. You'll be glad you did!

Call 1-780-736-0009 to connect with Bob 'Idea Man' Hooey today!

Learn more about Bob at: www.ideaman.net

"There is no such thing as a self made man or woman. You will reach your goals only with the help of others." George Shin This is where the time you invest working with your individual team members pays amazing dividends.

Japanese 23rd Psalm

*When stress overwhelms you, the Japanese
version of the 23rd Psalm can be very helpful*

The Lord is my Pacesetter, I shall not rush.
He makes me stop for quiet intervals;
He provides me with pictures of stillness,
Which restores my serenity.
He leads me in the way of efficiency through
calmness of mind, His guidance is peace.
Even though I have a great many things to
accomplish each day, I will not fret,
for His presence is with me.
His timelessness, His importance,
will keep me in balance.
He prepares refreshment and renewal in
the midst of any activity by annointing me
with the oil of his tranquility.
My cup of joyous energy overflows.
Surely harmony and effectiveness
shall be the fruit of my hours, and I
shall walk in the pace of the Lord,
and dwell in
His house forever.

Author Unknown

Thought we'd leave you with this stylized version of the 23rd Psalm. I've
shared this with audiences around the globe for their reflection.

Made in the USA
Charleston, SC
23 September 2014